THE DRIFT MODEL

How Claims Degrade Under Transmission Pressure

Zachary Handa · Georg Sinn

DEMETER ACADEMY PRESS · 2026

The Drift Model: How Claims Degrade Under Transmission Pressure

Published by Demeter Academy Press, Los Angeles

For permissions, inquiries, and additional resources, visit:
www.DemeterAcademy.com

Interior Design & Typesetting: Demeter Academy Press
Printed in the United States of America

ISBN: 978-1-971093-02-4
First edition, 2026

ANSWER ENGINE
J O U R N A L

This book was produced by **Answer Engine Journal**—an applied research and practitioner-focused publication dedicated to understanding how claims become visible, trusted, and repeated in AI-mediated information environments.

Answer Engine Journal examines the mechanics of selection, verification, and institutional legibility across search engines, answer engines, and public knowledge systems. Its work focuses on how explanations stabilize, how authority is conferred, and how incentives shape what becomes retrievable and actionable.

The Drift Model is intended as a durable reference. It does not rely on ongoing updates, companion tools, or supplemental materials to be used as designed. The model presented here is descriptive rather than tactical, and is meant to support diagnosis rather than optimization.

Related research, essays, and future publications are maintained at the Answer Engine Journal site.

The canonical hub for these materials is:

AnswerEngineJournal.com

Answer Engine Journal operates as an independent publication focused on the emerging discipline of answer-engine-mediated knowledge—built for environments where claims must survive selection pressure, institutional scrutiny, and machine-legible retrieval.

Acknowledgements

This book was developed over an extended period of observation, testing, and revision. It benefited from many conversations, critiques, and practical constraints that shaped both the model and its limits.

We are grateful to the researchers, analysts, journalists, editors, and institutional practitioners who were willing to think out loud with us—often in unfinished form—and who helped surface where the model clarified reality and where it failed to account for lived complexity. Many of these exchanges took place off the record; their value lies in the pressure they applied rather than in attribution.

We also thank the colleagues and peers who challenged early drafts, especially those who pushed back on scope, terminology, and misuse risk. Their insistence on restraint improved the book materially.

Several case studies benefited from domain-specific expertise. While responsibility for interpretation remains ours, the factual grounding and boundary conditions were sharpened through those contributions.

Finally, we acknowledge the institutions and systems—formal and informal—that made sustained, careful work possible. Time, silence, and the ability to revise without performance pressure are not neutral conditions. This book exists in part because those conditions were available.

Any errors, oversights, or misjudgments remain our own.

CONTENTS

THE MECHANICS OF DRIFT

THE FIVE STAGES OF DRIFT

BIBLIOGRAPHY

INTRODUCTION

Why This Book Exists Now

Public knowledge is undergoing a structural transformation.

A claim often begins inside a serious discipline—medicine, economics, public policy—bounded by evidence, scope, and caveats. As it moves into public circulation, its form changes. It becomes simpler, louder, and more confident. Constraints fall away. Scope expands. The versions that circulate most widely are shaped for ease of repetition, defense, and group alignment.

Common explanations focus on individual actors. Attention is placed on motives, incentives, or moral failures. Platforms are treated as distorting forces; audiences as disengaged or credulous. These accounts describe familiar surface features, but they do not explain why similar patterns recur across topics, institutions, and communities.

This book advances a structural diagnosis. Drift emerges from selection pressure.

Public knowledge now moves through environments that reward speed, certainty, and alignment. Claims that travel quickly are those that compress nuance. Claims that compete successfully for attention sharpen their edges. Claims that hold groups together take on signaling functions. Over time, the versions that persist reflect what the environment amplifies rather than what evidence most carefully supports.

Digital networks altered the conditions under which ideas circulate. Transmission costs collapsed, making distribution easy, while competition for attention intensified. In this landscape, claims evolve toward stickiness, recognizability, and social utility. They are shaped to be repeated, defended, and shared within groups.

These pressures produce consistent effects. Complexity slows transmission. Uncertainty introduces social risk. Moral clarity offers status and cohesion. As these forces accumulate, claims gradually separate from the evidentiary structures that once constrained them.

This book provides a model for understanding that process.

The purpose of the model is diagnostic. It treats drift as an engineering problem. The focus is on mechanics: how constraints degrade, how costs shape selection, and where intervention remains feasible.

This book is written for those who hold judgment under pressure—analysts, researchers, journalists, and institutional stewards who must interpret contested information environments. It is designed as a practical framework for seeing clearly when conditions favor distortion over accuracy.

How to Use This Guide

This book is built to be used, not just read.

It presents a descriptive model for how claims change function as they move through public circulation. Different readers will come to it with different roles, constraints, and time horizons. This section is intended to help you decide where to begin, how to move through the material, and how to use the model without turning it into an argument or a position.

WHO THIS BOOK IS FOR

You'll get the most value from this book if your work requires interpreting claims under pressure—often before full clarity is available.

This includes:

- **Researchers, analysts, or journalists** working with contested claims where accuracy, scope, and updateability matter more than persuasion.

- **Institutional stewards** in policy, education, public health, governance, trust & safety, or communications, responsible for decisions that must hold up under scrutiny.

- **Organizational leaders and operators** working inside KPI, strategy, or incentive systems where explanations harden into narratives and internal "truths."

- **Writers, editors, or educators** translating complex material into public-facing forms without losing constraint or calibration.

You do not need to share a political orientation, disciplinary background, or ideological framework. The model focuses on mechanics: transmission cost, selection pressure, and the ways social environments shape what claims become.

If you are looking for debunking, advocacy, or a toolkit for winning disputes, this book will feel intentionally indirect.

HOW THIS BOOK IS STRUCTURED

This book is organized to move from model construction to application, without requiring linear reading in all cases.

Each part serves a distinct function.

Parts I–III establish the model.

These sections define the unit of analysis (claims in motion), introduce the governing variable (transmission cost), and describe the five-stage drift pipeline alongside the selection pressures that shape movement between stages. Together, they provide the conceptual foundation required to recognize drift as a structural process rather than a failure of intent or belief.

Part IV applies the model through forensic case studies.

Each case traces a specific claim as it moves through public circulation. The emphasis is on auditing structural change—how constraints fall away, how social function shifts, and where revision becomes costly. These cases are not arguments and do not aim to resolve factual disputes. They demonstrate how the model operates across domains.

Part V provides a constrained toolkit.

This section is designed for use under pressure. It includes stage-locating guides, diagnostic checklists, and design considerations for reducing drift without turning the model into a status or identity instrument. The tools are intentionally bounded and should be treated as aids to judgment rather than decision rules.

Readers may move through these sections in different orders depending on need. The structure is designed to support both deep understanding and practical diagnosis, without collapsing the distinction between explanation and application.

READING FOR UNDERSTANDING

In this mode, the book functions as a conceptual framework.

Parts I–III are designed to be read in sequence. Together, they establish the unit of analysis (claims in motion), introduce the governing variable (transmission cost), describe the five-stage drift pipeline, and map the selection pressures that move claims between stages.

When reading this way, it helps to keep three disciplines in view:

- Treat examples as illustrative rather than comprehensive.

- Attend to mechanisms and incentives more than conclusions.

- Track what changes at each stage: what persists, what falls away, and what becomes costly to revise.

This mode is most useful for readers whose work involves interpretation and judgment.

USING THE MODEL UNDER CONSTRAINT

In this mode, the book functions as an operational reference.

Readers working under time or attention pressure can begin with Part V and the appendices. The one-page models, checklists, and worksheets are designed to support rapid audits of claims already in circulation. Outputs should be treated as provisional diagnostics rather than final determinations.

Once immediate pressure has passed, earlier chapters provide the context and nuance required for deeper judgment.

Scope and Misuse Boundary

This book presents a descriptive model for how claims change function as they move through environments that reward speed, clarity, safety, and repeatability. Its purpose is to make structural transformation visible—not to settle every dispute that drifted claims may later support.

Use the Drift Model as a diagnostic lens for structure: how constraints fall away, how incentives select for cheaper variants, and how claims acquire social function over time. Do not use it as a shortcut for deciding what is true, who is right, or which side deserves authority.

SCOPE (WHAT THIS MODEL IS FOR)

The Drift Model is designed to help you:

- Identify where a claim lost constraints as it traveled.

- Distinguish bounded claims from extracts, stories, and social objects.

- Map the selection pressures that reward simplification, certainty, and portability.

- Explain why drift persists even among competent, well-intentioned participants.

- Audit organizations, media systems, and communities for proxy capture and narrative hardening.

- Design limited defenses: where to add friction, preserve provenance, or refuse scale.

The model operates at the level of claims in motion, not beliefs held in isolation.

Non-Scope (What This Model Is Not For)

The Drift Model does not:

- Determine whether a claim is true or false. It explains transformation, not correctness.

- Diagnose intelligence, intent, or moral character. Drift is an environmental selection effect, not a personality trait.

- Assign blame by default. It describes pressures and outcomes, not hidden motives.

- Replace domain expertise, evidence review, or verification practices.

- Function as a general theory of culture, ideology, or belief writ large.

If you are looking for debunking, persuasion, or a method for winning disputes, this model will feel deliberately incomplete.

Misuse Boundary (When the Model Breaks)

The Drift Model fails when it is used to sort people rather than analyze structure.

Common misuse patterns include:

- **Status labeling:** treating stage language as an insult or identity marker rather than a descriptive state.

- **Shortcut certainty:** declaring "this is drift" to avoid engaging underlying evidence or uncertainty.

- **Asymmetric application:** diagnosing drift in out-groups while exempting one's own community or institution.

- **Totalizing explanation:** using drift to explain everything, which removes its discriminative power.

- **Just-so narratives:** retrofitting events to the model

without specifying pressures, constraints, or alternative explanations.

When the model becomes a badge, a weapon, or a performance of sophistication, it has already drifted.

MINIMUM STANDARD FOR USE

A valid application of the Drift Model includes:

1. The original claim, stated as narrowly and bounded as possible.

2. The transmission path: where it traveled and through which formats.

3. The dominant pressures shaping that environment.

4. The specific transformations observed: what constraints fell away and what replaced them.

5. A falsifier: what would make the diagnosis incorrect.

If these elements cannot be specified, treat the output as a hypothesis, not a conclusion.

Definitions and Notation

The book relies on a small set of recurring terms with specific meanings. These are operational definitions: they function as diagnostic handles rather than philosophical positions.

These definitions are not exhaustive. They fix how terms are used in this book so that later analysis can proceed without re-litigating meaning.

DRIFT

Drift refers to the systematic degradation of claims under transmission pressure.

Drift emerges from structural conditions rather than individual motive. It can occur even when participants are well intentioned, and it can affect claims that are accurate at the point of origin. Repeated circulation changes what is carried forward, what is dropped, and what becomes difficult to revise.

TRANSMISSION COST

Transmission cost is the total cognitive, social, and technical effort required to carry a claim's constraints intact across audiences and contexts.

That cost is always paid by someone: speakers invest time and risk, listeners invest attention and cognitive load, and institutions invest verification and enforcement. Over time, cost shapes selection. Lower-cost variants tend to spread and stabilize, even when higher-cost variants preserve greater accuracy.

SELECTION ENVIRONMENT

A selection environment is the incentive landscape that shapes which claims spread, which stabilize, and which resist correction.

Platforms function as environments defined by reward structures rather than as intentional agents. Because environments are designed, their pressures can be shifted. Later chapters treat format, norms, routing, and friction as variables that alter selection dynamics.

UPDATE RESISTANCE

Update resistance is the expected social cost of revising a claim, including identity entanglement and potential status loss.

As claims move through stages, update resistance tends to increase. Later-stage claims are often bound to belonging, loyalty, and rank, which helps explain why disconfirming information is frequently processed as threat rather than signal.

FALSIFIABILITY

Falsifiability refers to the clarity of conditions under which a claim would require revision or abandonment.

A claim may be falsifiable in principle while remaining resistant in practice when social costs make disconfirmation inert. In the tools, falsifiability functions as a diagnostic axis: low falsifiability combined with high update resistance produces a consistent risk profile.

EPISTEMIC INFRASTRUCTURE

Epistemic infrastructure consists of the institutions, norms, and tools that govern how claims are produced, constrained, corrected, and archived.

Historically, accuracy prevailed not through philosophy alone but through infrastructural support—routing, friction, and validation pathways. The objective in this book is partial restoration of correction capacity: strengthening update pathways while maintaining bounded scope and proportionality.

NOTATION CONVENTIONS

- After first introduction, stages are referenced numerically as Stage 1 through Stage 5.

- Danger-to-calibration (where used) denotes claims that combine high update resistance with low falsifiability.

- Icons and symbols in one-page models serve as shorthand and are defined at first appearance.

The Drift Model: A Structural Overview

The Drift Model describes how claims change function as they move through public circulation. These changes are not random. Under stable selection pressures, claims tend to pass through a small number of recognizable configurations. Each stage is defined less by what people believe than by what the claim is used for.

What follows is a compact description of those stages and the pressures that move claims between them.

STAGE 1: SERIOUS TRADITIONS

At Stage 1, claims function as bounded models. They circulate within communities that share standards for evidence, calibration, and correction. Constraints travel with the proposition: scope conditions, uncertainty, and falsifiers are considered part of the claim rather than optional context.

The dominant pressure here is calibration. Accuracy is maintained through formal update routes—peer review, training, revision norms, and institutional memory. Drift at this stage is slow and usually appears at boundaries, where translation into other contexts introduces error.

STAGE 2: MEME EXTRACTS

As claims move into broader circulation, they are compressed for portability. What survives is a handle: a phrase, image, or simplified proposition that can be easily repeated and recognized.

Constraints begin to fall away. Transmission cost drops. Shareability becomes the dominant pressure, and low-cost variants gain an advantage even when they preserve less of the original model. Correction is still possible, often through link-backs or constraint-preserving summaries, but those pathways depend on norms that are increasingly fragile.

The characteristic failure mode at this stage is qualifier stripping and scope ambiguity.

STAGE 3: FOLK THEORIES

At Stage 3, extracts cohere into a story. The claim now functions as an explanatory system that provides closure and interpretive convenience. Gaps and uncertainty are smoothed over. A monoculture narrative forms.

Selection pressure shifts toward coherence. Competing explanations are evaluated less on evidentiary fit and more on whether they disrupt the story. Correction becomes harder because it must now compete with a complete explanatory frame rather than a single proposition.

Drift here takes the form of causal collapse and declining falsifiability.

STAGE 4: STATUS ENGINES

At Stage 4, claims become performative. Fluency with the framework signals competence. Public alignment establishes rank. The claim's primary function is no longer explanation but social sorting.

Selection pressure favors certainty and confidence. Correction threatens status and is often handled privately, if at all. What looks like debate is frequently competence theater: escalation through sharper stances, purer interpretations, and more visible commitment.

Failure modes include purity spirals and performative escalation.

STAGE 5: IDENTITY SYSTEMS

At Stage 5, claims stabilize as identity markers. They define belonging and enforce boundaries. Nuance becomes dangerous. Disagreement reads as betrayal.

Exit costs are high. Revision threatens relationships, status, and self-concept. Correction pathways are largely closed, and off-ramps depend on changes to the surrounding social environment rather than new information.

Drift at this stage is maintained through taboo enforcement, heresy categories, and immunization against disconfirming evidence.

TRANSITIONS AND PRESSURES

Movement between stages is driven by shifts in selection pressure:

- From **Stage 1 to Stage 2**, compression for portability dominates. Shareability begins to outweigh constraint fidelity.

- From **Stage 2 to Stage 3**, explanatory closure dominates. Coherence begins to outweigh uncertainty.

- From **Stage 3 to Stage 4**, social sorting dominates. Performative competence begins to outweigh accuracy.

- From **Stage 4 to Stage 5**, exit cost dominates. Loyalty begins to outweigh revision.

These pressures operate independently of intent. Well-meaning participants can accelerate drift simply by responding rationally to the environment they inhabit.

READING THE MODEL

The model is best used descriptively. Locate the stage a claim is functioning in, identify the dominant pressure acting on it, and consider what kinds of interventions are viable at that layer. Early-stage interventions restore constraints. Late-stage interventions focus on lowering social cost and reopening exit pathways.

Used this way, the model clarifies why some corrections succeed, why others fail, and why timing matters more than argument quality.

PART I

The Mechanics of Drift

Scroll through a social feed, listen to a political debate, or read a viral thread on health, and a familiar pattern appears. A complex reality—a medical study, a legislative bill, a historical event— arrives in compressed form. Nuance falls away. Probabilities settle into certainties.

As claims move beyond their point of origin, they enter environments shaped by speed, competition, and limited attention. Context thins. Formats reward brevity. Distribution systems privilege material that can be repeated quickly and recognized easily. Under these conditions, claims do not persist because they are careful. They persist because they move.

This book treats that pattern as a structural phenomenon. The degradation of information follows from selection pressure. When bounded claims circulate through high-velocity channels, the versions that survive tend to be those with the lowest transmission cost.

Drift is the name given to this process. It describes the predictable way complex claims shed constraints as they pass through public circulation. What remains is not necessarily false. It is adapted for speed, repetition, and social compatibility rather than for carrying the full structure that originally supported its accuracy.

The purpose of Part I is to establish the foundations of that model. Across the first three chapters, the focus shifts from intent to environment, and from individual actors to the pressures acting on claims in motion.

Chapter 1 (The Problem) describes the selection environment. It examines how speed, competition, and context loss generate transmission pressure, and why low-cost variants tend to outcompete more carefully bounded versions.

Chapter 2 (The Hidden Variable) introduces transmission cost as the central driver of drift. It explains why accuracy is heavy—requiring time, attention, and social risk to maintain—and why compressed variants are lighter and therefore more competitive as circulation accelerates.

Chapter 3 (The Unit of Analysis) turns to the object itself. It defines the claim bundle: the combination of scope, substrate, and constraints that make a statement function as intended. From this perspective, drift is not a change in wording alone. It is the systematic loss of the structures that once traveled with the claim.

By the end of Part I, a viral headline should register differently. Rather than appearing simply right or wrong, it can be seen as an object shaped by pressure—compressed, smoothed, and optimized by the pipeline it has just moved through.

CHAPTER 1

The Problem: Knowledge Under Transmission Pressure

Across health, politics, technology, and finance, knowledge increasingly moves under compression.

Complex realities are shaped into short forms, fast cycles, and competitive environments where mobility determines survival. Claims leave the lab or the newsroom early. They stabilize in public circulation before boundary conditions are fully articulated. By the time corrections arrive, the claims have already acquired weight and inertia.

A common response is to search for culprits: bad actors, careless audiences, or cultural decline. A more consistent explanation sits elsewhere. Transmission pressure—the combined effect of speed, competition, and context loss—acts on claims as they circulate. Under this pressure, low-cost versions reliably outpace high-cost ones. Qualifiers fall away. Scope expands. Bounded propositions transform into portable objects: easy to repeat and increasingly resistant to revision.

In this book, pressure refers to an environmental property.

High-velocity networks impose a selection dynamic in which fitness is determined by mobility rather than accuracy. Attention scarcity rewards speed. Ranking systems privilege performance. Remix culture treats claims as material to be clipped, simplified, and reused. Distribution channels do more than carry knowledge; they shape it. The ideas that persist tend to be those that move smoothly through the system.

This produces a subtle but consequential shift. Two questions begin to converge: *"Is this true?"* and *"Will this spread?"* Under pressure, spreadability is resolved first. By the time accuracy receives sustained attention, the claim has already settled into place. It has become part of the social landscape, structured around repetition and reinforcement.

This dynamic is often discussed under the banner of "misinformation," a frame that emphasizes the separation of falsehood from fact. A structural view reveals a broader process. As claims circulate, they acquire additional functions. They operate as signals, shortcuts, rallying points, or badges of belonging. In these roles, they move through social space as currency as much as information.

Accuracy alone does not prevent this transformation. Claims can begin fully correct and still degrade. When truth depends on heavy constraints—specific contexts, limited scope, careful assumptions—those constraints carry high transmission cost. As circulation accelerates, the core proposition remains while the structure that sustained its accuracy thins. Drift emerges as a routine outcome of moving bounded knowledge through environments optimized for low-cost repetition.

This pathway appears across domains and cultures. Technical communities explaining AI risk encounter the same compression dynamics as wellness spaces promoting health protocols. The language changes; the pressure remains constant. Ideas shed constraints, consolidate into simple explanations, and gradually take on social roles that stabilize them in place. The mechanism operates independently of content.

This structural account also clarifies why correction grows difficult over time. It is a problem of weight. A circulating claim is light: concise, confident, and easy to pass along. A responsible correction carries context—scope limits, uncertainty, competing evidence. That added structure increases cost in environments tuned for ease and speed.

As circulation continues, another cost accumulates: the social cost of updating. Early revisions feel like refinement. Later revisions interact with status and belonging. Once a claim signals competence or group alignment, new information changes its meaning. Revision becomes socially consequential.

The chapters that follow provide a way to observe these transformations without moral escalation. The model introduced here offers a vocabulary for locating claims within their lifecycle. We trace a predictable sequence: claims move from **Serious Traditions** into **Meme Extracts**, consolidate into **Folk Theories**, convert into **Status Engines**, and, in some cases, harden into **Identity Systems**. The task is to understand how information behaves under sustained pressure—and how environments shape what knowledge becomes.

CHAPTER 2

Transmission Cost as the Hidden Variable

Public debates about belief formation often start from individual traits: intelligence, education, seriousness, or intent. A more reliable explanation lies elsewhere. Claims move through environments that reward some forms of expression over others. To understand drift, the relevant question is what it costs to believe—and to transmit—different versions of the same claim.

Under transmission pressure, every claim competes with alternatives that are easier to carry. Ease here refers to efficiency. A low-cost claim requires less time to explain, less attention to process, fewer qualifications to track, and less reputational risk to repeat. In fast, crowded environments, these efficient variants consistently outrun heavier ones, even among highly capable people.

This pattern explains why simplified explanations spread, why experts repeat confident summaries, and why familiar frames persist even when their limits are widely understood. The driver is cost minimization. When an environment rewards speed, clarity, and social safety, the version of a claim that survives is the one that can be expressed, defended, and repeated at the lowest total price.

Transmission cost is a useful lens because it explains drift without assigning blame. It accounts for why accurate claims lose fidelity, why caveats fall away, and why correction often requires sustained effort. It also reveals leverage. When drift follows cost gradients, effective intervention focuses on altering those gradients—lowering the cost of carrying constraints or increasing the cost of distortion.

Before examining the stages of drift, it helps to specify the currency of the system. Transmission cost is a bundle rather than a single factor. It reflects the total price—paid in attention, time, status, and friction—required to move a claim with its constraints intact.

That bundle consistently includes four components.

Cognitive cost refers to the mental load required to understand a claim. When a non-expert struggles to restate a proposition accurately after limited exposure, the cognitive cost is high.

Time cost reflects the amount of setup required to make a claim safe to repeat. Statements that require extended threads, lectures, or background reading before they can be shared reliably carry higher time costs.

Social cost captures the reputational consequences of expressing uncertainty. In many environments, confident assertion increases status, while hedging or conditional language reduces it. Over time, this dynamic favors claims that minimize visible uncertainty.

Technical cost arises from the medium itself. Character limits, ranking systems, thumbnails, and recommendation incentives all privilege claims that compress cleanly and penalize those that rely on extended context.

Together, these costs give drift its direction. When accurate versions of a claim are expensive to carry, lower-cost variants gain an advantage. The burden of maintaining scope and conditions often shifts as a claim travels. What begins with a researcher or institution arrives downstream as a polished object. The work of checking limits and assumptions is transferred to the audience. Most audiences route instead by fluency, repetition, or social proof.

Correction moves along the same gradient. Revising a claim requires additional time, attention, and tolerance for ambiguity. In high-speed systems, those requirements reduce uptake. As a result, multiple interpretations compete primarily on efficiency rather than accuracy.

Each qualifier adds cognitive load. Each hedge adds time. Each signal of uncertainty increases social risk. As these costs accumulate, high-fidelity versions become heavy, while simplified versions move lightly. Selection favors the latter because lighter objects travel farther and faster.

Claims shed weight through recurring compression moves. These moves increase portability without requiring deception. Qualifier stripping removes conditions that slow repetition. Narrative substitution replaces complex causal models with simpler stories. Moral clarity substitution trades uncertainty for judgment. Anecdote substitution allows a vivid case to stand in for a general pattern. Binary conversion turns probabilities into switches. Normative capture transforms descriptions into prescriptions.

These compressions make drift directional. Constraint fidelity is exchanged for portability. Once a low-cost version stabilizes, revision requires moving uphill against the cost gradient. Early variants gain a head start through repetition and familiarity and often become the baseline against which later corrections must compete.

The dynamic can be summarized as a practical heuristic:

When a claim depends on constraints to remain accurate, and those constraints are costly to transmit, drift pressure increases.

This holds regardless of where a claim originates. When accuracy depends on caveats, scope limits, or probabilistic reasoning—and those elements carry weight—the system favors cheaper substitutes. Drift follows predictable selection dynamics. Addressing it requires cost engineering: designing environments where carrying constraints becomes easier and distortion becomes expensive.

CHAPTER 3

What Exactly Drifts

Before drift can be diagnosed, the moving object has to be specified with care. Precision at this stage determines the clarity of everything that follows. When the unit of analysis is well defined, later explanations remain grounded rather than sliding into moral interpretation.

Many discussions of information quality begin with ideas. Ideas, however, are diffuse. They combine values, intuitions, and narratives into a single mental field. Their boundaries are porous, and their failure conditions are hard to locate. When an idea changes, it is often unclear what shifted or why. Studying drift requires an object that can be traced, compared, and audited.

The relevant object is a claim.

More precisely, it is a **claim bundle**.

A claim functions as more than a sentence. It includes the supporting structure that allows the sentence to remain accurate across contexts. It can be understood as a package with multiple components. At its center is the proposition—the headline statement being asserted. Surrounding that proposition are the constraints that keep it true. These typically include scope, which specifies where and when the claim applies; substrate, which identifies the kind of evidence or method supporting it; and falsifiers, which define the conditions under which the claim would require revision or abandonment.

Within serious traditions, these elements move together. Repeating a finding responsibly involves repeating the context that bounds it. As long as the bundle remains intact, accuracy is preserved through shared standards and update pathways.

As claims enter higher-pressure environments, the conditions of movement change. Carrying the full bundle becomes costly, and transmission favors lighter forms.

This shift introduces the core mechanism of drift: **constraint shedding**.

The process is straightforward and observable. The proposition continues forward, while the bundle loosens. When a claim moves from contexts that can hold complexity—research papers, technical manuals, classrooms—into environments optimized for speed and reach, each additional constraint adds friction. The proposition fits easily into a headline or post. Scope requires extra words. Substrate requires citations. Falsifiers interrupt momentum.

As circulation accelerates, constraints drop away. The headline separates from the fine print.

This shedding follows recurring patterns. Qualifiers contract, turning conditional language into declarative statements. Probabilistic findings solidify into facts, as certainty travels more efficiently than uncertainty. Scope expands, converting local observations into general rules. Studies of specific populations become claims about human behavior at large. Mechanism substitution replaces correlation with causation, because causal stories are easier to remember and retell than statistical relationships.

The most consequential change occurs when falsifiers disappear. In the original bundle, clear conditions indicated when the claim would fail. As drift progresses, those conditions fade from view. Disconfirming evidence is absorbed as noise, bias, or exception. The claim persists, not because it has grown more robust, but because the mechanisms that enabled revision have thinned.

Claims also change through legitimate development. Evidence accumulates. Definitions sharpen. Explanations gain precision. These forms of evolution typically add weight to the bundle by increasing constraint density and narrowing scope. Drift moves in a different direction. It reduces carrying cost and increases speed, favoring portability over fidelity.

This dynamic explains why drifted claims often feel compelling.

They appear clearer, bolder, and easier to use. Their performance in public circulation improves as constraints fall away, even though those same constraints once maintained accuracy.

By treating the claim bundle as the unit of analysis, attention shifts away from explanations centered on intelligence or intent. Constraint shedding emerges as an adaptive response to environments that reward lightness. Participants select the version of the claim that travels most easily under prevailing pressures.

With the object now specified and the force already introduced in the previous chapter, the next step is to map where shedding occurs. The movement follows a recognizable path. Claims travel from bounded traditions into portable forms and, under sustained pressure, consolidate into systems that increasingly resist revision.

PART II
The Five Stages of Drift

If Part I described the environment, Part II traces movement through it.

Across the next five chapters, a single claim is followed as it leaves a high-friction setting—a laboratory, a technical text, a formal discipline—and enters wider public circulation. At each step, the claim changes. Constraints fall away, speed increases, and new social functions emerge.

This movement follows a consistent pattern shaped by the pressures described in Part I. Each stage represents a stable configuration: a way a claim functions once it has adapted to a particular incentive structure.

Chapter 4 (Stage 1: Serious Traditions) begins at the point of origin. Claims are produced and maintained within shared standards of training, review, and correction. Accuracy is supported by dense constraints and formal update pathways.

Chapter 5 (Stage 2: Meme Extracts) marks the point of extraction. Claims are compressed into portable forms that travel easily through attention-driven environments.

Chapter 6 (Stage 3: Folk Theories) follows the recombination of fragments into coherent explanations. Communities assemble "good enough" stories that provide interpretive closure and shared understanding.

Chapter 7 (Stage 4: Status Engines) tracks the shift from explanation to competition. Claims begin to signal competence, fluency, and rank within a social field.

Chapter 8 (Stage 5: Identity Systems) describes the endpoint of the pipeline. Claims stabilize as moral boundaries, where belief primarily organizes belonging and alignment.

Throughout this section, the focus is on function rather than factual status. A Stage 5 claim may remain technically accurate while operating primarily as a signal. A Stage 2 claim may remain useful while functioning as a handle rather than a full model.

Understanding drift therefore requires more than evaluating correctness. It also requires attention to role: what the claim is doing, what pressures shape it, and what costs accompany revision. This section provides the conceptual tools needed to locate a claim within the pipeline and to diagnose the forces acting on it.

CHAPTER 4

Stage 1: Serious Traditions

We begin where claims begin: inside environments designed to hold them together.

Stage 1 describes a claim before it has been optimized for travel. The primary objective at this stage is stability. Claims circulating inside a serious tradition are supported by infrastructure that preserves coherence. Methods remain attached to conclusions. Boundary conditions travel with the proposition. Criteria for revision are explicit and legible.

These environments sustain precision through friction. Participants are trained to treat constraints as integral to the claim rather than as optional context. Restating a conclusion without its limits prompts correction. Competence is signaled through calibration. The governing norm is updateability.

We refer to these environments as **serious traditions**. The term identifies systems organized to preserve constraint fidelity. A serious tradition may take many forms: a research lab, a standards body, a monastery, or an open-source engineering community. What unites them is infrastructure rather than ideology or prestige.

Across domains, these traditions share a common set of mechanical features.

They maintain trained interpretive norms. Members learn how to read, restate, and transmit claims before participating in circulation.

They operate with shared standards of evidence. Disagreement occurs within a framework that specifies what constitutes support, refutation, and revision.

They preserve institutional memory. Errors are recorded. Retractions remain visible. Past claims shape how new ones are evaluated.

They impose costs for imprecision. Overstating a finding reduces standing within the community.

Together, these features function as stabilizers. By raising the cost of transmission, they keep the claim bundle intact.

Bounded claims at Stage 1 rely on explicit scope conditions. They specify where the claim applies and how it could fail. Interpretive training aligns participants on how to handle uncertainty. Friction—peer review, apprenticeship, slow publication cycles— filters low-fidelity variants before they outrun accurate ones. Institutional memory anchors new claims to prior evidence.

When these stabilizers are in place, what circulates is a complete claim bundle. The proposition travels alongside its substrate and falsifiers. Participants understand the claim's strength, its limits, and the conditions under which it would change. Revision is routine maintenance rather than reputational crisis.

This stability carries a tradeoff. Stage 1 claims are heavy. They move slowly and require training to use well. That weight becomes salient at the boundary.

Transitions out of Stage 1 occur at interfaces.

One interface is attention. Under time constraint, compression favors conclusions over calibration, allowing the proposition to advance.

Another interface is translation. When specialists communicate with journalists, policymakers, or executives, incentives shift. The receiver prioritizes clarity and relevance. When the full claim bundle exceeds what can be carried across the gap, simplification follows.

A third interface is novelty. Outside the tradition, speed and decisiveness are rewarded. Clear summaries travel further than careful ones.

These pressures initiate the transition to Stage 2. The governing question shifts. Instead of asking whether a claim remains fully bounded, the environment asks whether it can be repeated without training.

To move beyond the boundary, the claim sheds weight. The proposition stands alone. Substrate falls away. Falsifiers recede. What remains is the smallest version of the claim that a stranger can carry.

This transition reflects transmission cost. As circulation accelerates, the claim becomes an extract.

From this point on, the claim is no longer evaluated primarily within individual understanding; it enters circulation, where selection pressure replaces judgment as the dominant force.

CHAPTER 5

Stage 2: Meme Extracts

Stage 1 preserves a claim within a serious tradition. Stage 2 allows it to move.

As a claim leaves its origin context, it enters an environment governed by a different question. The central pressure is no longer preservation, but carriage. The environment asks whether an idea can travel—whether it can be parsed quickly, repeated easily, and recognized at a glance. Survival in high-velocity circulation requires compression.

This is the process of **meme extraction**.

In this book, a meme refers to a functional unit rather than a specific format. A meme extract is any compressed object engineered for transmission.[1] It may appear as a quote card, a headline, a short clip, a slogan, or a "one simple trick." The form varies. The function remains the same. A meme extract carries an idea without carrying the full structure that originally supported it. It functions as a handle: a lightweight grip that allows an idea to be passed along with minimal effort.

Compression at this stage is inevitable. Complex claims cannot move intact through fast, crowded channels. At the same time, compression creates pressure on fidelity. Constraints carry weight. Qualifiers, scope limits, and falsifiers slow movement. Under transmission pressure, they tend to fall away first.

This erosion follows a small set of recurring compression moves.

Qualifier stripping converts probability into certainty. "May" becomes "is." "Evidence suggests" becomes "science proves." The proposition remains recognizable, while the uncertainty that

---

1   Limor Shifman, *Memes in Digital Culture* (Cambridge, MA: MIT Press, 2014), chapters defining internet memes, spreadability, and how remix/compression alters meaning and function.

stabilized it is removed.

Scope expansion turns a local finding into a general rule. A result drawn from a specific population becomes a statement about people in general. Limits dissolve because broad claims travel more easily.

Narrative substitution replaces a complex mechanism with a simple takeaway. The audience receives a conclusion without the path that produced it. Process condenses into outcome.

Moral tagging attaches a stance. The extract communicates how the claim should be felt—urgent, dangerous, virtuous, corrupt. Endorsement becomes socially legible without engaging the underlying logic.

Evidence laundering preserves the appearance of authority while reducing the substrate. A vague reference to a study or expert stands in for explanation. The citation operates as a seal rather than a route back to the source.

These extracts succeed because they fit the environment. They are quick to understand, easy to repeat, and immediately legible as social signals. In attention-driven systems, those advantages consistently outweigh losses in precision. A vivid, incomplete slogan tends to outrun a complete, careful explanation.

Stage 2 remains unstable. It represents a fork rather than a destination.

In one path, an extract functions as a heuristic. It simplifies while signaling its own incompleteness. It lowers the cost of entry and preserves a visible route back to the source. Used this way, Stage 2 widens access while keeping correction viable.

In the other path, the extract begins to substitute for the underlying claim. The handle becomes the object. The slogan is treated as the whole reality. Instead of opening inquiry, it provides closure. The fragment starts to organize perception, shaping what is noticed and what is ignored.

This pressure sets up the next transition. Extracts remain fragments only briefly. As they accumulate, demand for coherence grows. The environment favors assembly. Discrete pieces are drawn together into a story that explains what is happening.

This is how a portable extract consolidates into a Folk Theory.

CHAPTER 6
Stage 3: Folk Theory

Stage 2 produces fragments—memes, slogans, and headlines that move quickly. Stage 3 turns those fragments into a place to stand.

At this stage, a portable handle consolidates into a shared explanation. As a claim circulates widely, it begins to function as a lens for interpreting events. The governing pressure shifts from portability to closure. Partial truths are assembled into stories that feel complete enough to reduce uncertainty, assign meaning, and organize attention.

We call this structure a **folk theory**.

A folk theory is a functional adaptation. When high-fidelity expertise is difficult to access—whether because of jargon, institutional distance, or trust barriers—communities continue to explain the world by building substitutes that meet their needs. Stage 2 extracts are assembled into a system that can be shared, learned, and used collectively.

Folk theories persist because they solve a coordination problem. They provide a common frame that allows people to interpret events and communicate without renegotiating basic assumptions each time. Even in complex domains, the theory offers interpretive closure. It answers the question "What is going on here?" in a way that is fast, legible, and socially portable. Over time, it takes on the role of social infrastructure.

That stability emerges through a small set of predictable structural shifts.

First, the theory develops a monocausal orientation. Coordinating around complexity is difficult, so explanation converges on a single driver. One mechanism—capitalism, trauma, inflammation, the deep state—functions as a master key that links diverse outcomes into a unified story.

Second, boundaries widen. An explanation that begins in a specific context expands to cover adjacent cases, then broader domains. Scope generalizes as the theory proves useful across situations.

Third, the theory develops anecdote magnetism. It becomes a framework for sorting stories. News events, personal experiences, and viral clips are interpreted through the lens, reinforcing the frame and extending its reach.

Together, these shifts establish interpretive dominance. The theory becomes the default way of seeing. Competing frames fade from view, and disagreement is increasingly interpreted as misalignment with the shared understanding. The theory explains the world and provides an account of why others interpret it differently.

As this consolidation continues, evidence takes on a new role. Information that fits the story circulates easily and reinforces coherence. Information that complicates the picture requires additional effort to integrate. Information that challenges the frame is reinterpreted within the theory's logic. The structure becomes durable because it incorporates challenge into its own explanatory machinery.

One of the most consequential changes involves how uncertainty is treated. In bounded claims, uncertainty invites caution and further inquiry. In a folk theory, missing information is often incorporated as part of the explanation itself. Gaps acquire meaning. The theory closes by treating incompleteness as informative.

Alongside these epistemic shifts, a social change emerges. Repeating the theory begins to perform work for the speaker.

Fluency signals competence. It demonstrates familiarity with the shared frame and the ability to apply it quickly. Mastery becomes a proxy for insight. Endorsement signals alignment. Hesitation signals distance.

This is the hinge point. The claim continues to explain events, but it also begins to organize people. Once a theory distinguishes those who "get it" from those who do not, explanation and performance converge.

The selection pressure is preparing to shift again. In an environment where the theory is widely known, repetition loses its signaling power. Distinction requires use. The theory must begin to sort.

The implicit instruction evolves from "Make sense of the world" to "Locate who belongs where."

That evolution marks the transition to Stage 4.

CHAPTER 7

Stage 4: Status Engines

At Stage 4, a claim's primary function shifts. What once served as an explanation now operates as a ranking instrument.[2]

In Stage 3, the folk theory helped participants make sense of events. In Stage 4, it organizes social position. The governing function moves from interpretation to hierarchy maintenance. Truth and evidence remain part of the vocabulary, but the practical work of the claim is comparative: competent or incompetent, insider or outsider, reliable or suspect.

At this stage, the claim functions as a **status engine**.

What carries forward is a performable stance. The unit of analysis shifts from the claim itself to the ability to deploy it effectively. Fluency becomes the relevant signal. The practical question becomes whether the position can be expressed in the right way, at the right moment, for the right audience.

The environment consistently rewards three traits: speed, certainty, and aggression.

Speed functions as a signal of vigilance.

Certainty functions as a signal of strength.

Aggression compresses complexity into posture. Sharp judgment travels faster and performs better than careful qualification.

The dominant media formats at this stage reflect these incentives. Quote-posts, reaction clips, public call-outs, and "dunks" are optimized for visibility and evaluation. The addressed party matters less than the observing audience, who assess the

---

2   Whitney Phillips and Ryan M. Milner, *The Ambivalent Internet: Mischief, Oddity, and Antagonism Online* (Cambridge: Polity, 2017), chapters on antagonism/ambivalence and participatory dynamics that convert discourse into social sorting.

performance and assign rank.

Competence theater emerges as the organizing logic.

Within a status engine, participants develop the skills required to sound correct. They acquire the approved vocabulary, identify sanctioned adversaries, and learn the accepted diagnostics. Over time, performance substitutes for comprehension. Recognition accrues to those who signal alignment convincingly and consistently.

Once a claim is used to rank people, a second mechanism takes hold: incentive lock-in.

In earlier stages, revision functions as an epistemic update. At Stage 4, revision carries a visible social price. Shifting position reinterprets prior performances and alters standing among peers and allies.

This creates a reinforcing asymmetry. Public performance raises the cost of later adjustment. When reputation is built on early certainty or decisive judgment, subsequent nuance reads as retreat. The role itself constrains movement.

As a result, the system increasingly disfavors behaviors that complicate sorting. Neutrality fails to generate comparative signal. Steel-manning reduces contrast. Uncertainty interferes with spectacle and weakens ranking clarity.

Over time, constant comparison produces its own strain. Maintaining hierarchy through perpetual evaluation becomes costly. The environment adapts by changing the basis of sorting.

The central question shifts from *"Who demonstrates the greatest competence?"* to *"Who demonstrates reliable alignment?"*

This marks the escalation toward a moral boundary. Certain questions lose safety. Disagreement reorganizes into deviance. The claim's function shifts again, from displaying insight to signaling reliability and shared orientation.

At this point, the claim is approaching its next transformation: consolidation as identity.

STAGE 5: IDENTITY SYSTEMS • 25

CHAPTER 8

Stage 5: Identity Systems

Stage 5 represents the terminal configuration of the drift pipeline.

In Stage 4, claims functioned as tools. They were used to signal competence, establish rank, and compete in contests of fluency. Over time, sustained use alters the relationship between the person and the belief. The claim shifts from something a person deploys to something that organizes their position within a social system.

At Stage 5, the system resolves into **identity**. The claim operates as infrastructure: it organizes belonging, defines loyalty, and structures threat perception. Belief functions as a marker of membership rather than a proposition to be examined.

The governing function at this stage is cohesion. Where Stage 3 prioritized explanatory closure and Stage 4 prioritized social sorting, Stage 5 stabilizes group identity. The claim specifies who "we" are, what alignment looks like, and which positions fall outside the boundary. Accuracy recedes as a primary concern. Belonging becomes the dominant axis.

The transition from Stage 4 to Stage 5 is a qualitative shift. In a status system, participation and identity remain separable. A person can lose rank, face correction, or suffer reputational damage while remaining distinct from the game itself. In an identity system, that separation collapses. The belief integrates with character. Questioning the claim registers as defection rather than disagreement.

This integration changes the governing constraint. In earlier stages, transmission cost shaped which variants survived. In Stage 5, exit cost becomes the dominant force.

When a belief defines community, departure carries asymmetric consequences. Leaving often entails the loss of relationships sustained through shared affirmation. It can involve forfeiting status granted by the system, access to meaning, material support, or protection. These costs accumulate over time, reshaping the incentive landscape.

As exit costs rise, the system produces an exit lock. Belief revision becomes a social rupture rather than a cognitive update. Even private uncertainty acquires weight because it implies a future decision point. Persistence follows from cost structure: staying is cheaper than leaving.

To sustain this configuration, the system develops boundary mechanisms that regulate interpretation and participation.

One mechanism is taboo formation. Certain questions fall outside acceptable discourse. Silence around them reflects successful constraint rather than shared agreement.

Another mechanism is moral contamination. External ideas are treated as pollutants rather than competing explanations. Exposure itself carries risk, because the system prioritizes insulation over engagement.

A third mechanism takes the form of purification rituals. When ambiguity appears within the group, restoration of standing requires a visible act of realignment—an apology, clarification, or reaffirmation. The ritual signals cohesion more than content fidelity.

Together, these mechanisms produce interpretive stability. Conditions that once would have revised the claim are reclassified. External evidence arrives already coded as hostile. Internal dissent is processed as boundary stress. Interpretive authority concentrates around figures who translate events into group-safe meanings, allowing reality to be assimilated without destabilizing identity.

At this stage, interventions that rely on argument have limited effect. Challenges are processed as threats, and exposure tends to reinforce existing alignments. Interventions with leverage operate at the structural level: lowering the social cost of exit, creating face-saving pathways for revision, or providing private contexts where uncertainty can be held without immediate consequence.

The Completed Pipeline

The full arc of drift is now visible.

- It begins in **Stage 1 (Serious Traditions)**, where claims are stabilized by dense constraints and shared correction norms.

- It accelerates in **Stage 2 (Meme Extracts)**, where compression increases portability and reduces friction.

- It consolidates in **Stage 3 (Folk Theories)**, where fragments assemble into coherent explanations that favor closure.

- It intensifies in **Stage 4 (Status Engines)**, where claims function as instruments of ranking and performance.

- It stabilizes in **Stage 5 (Identity Systems)**, where belief operates as a protected boundary supported by high exit cost.

This sequence describes how information adapts to pressure. It tracks changes in function rather than changes in character.

Once the stage a claim occupies becomes visible, attention shifts from debating content to examining environment. The relevant question is no longer what to argue, but which pressures are sustaining the system—and which adjustments might reopen the possibility of revision.

PART III

The Selection Environment

In Part II, we followed the movement of a claim. We watched it shed constraints, consolidate into explanation, and harden into a social instrument.

The remaining question is why this pattern repeats so reliably. Why do claims drift in this direction, across domains and audiences?

The instinctive answer is to blame the people involved. Journalists are accused of carelessness, influencers of cynicism, audiences of gullibility. But replacing the participants does not change the outcome. When capable, well-intentioned people operate inside the same conditions, the same distortions reappear. The problem is not the player. It is the game.

Part III examines the game.

Across the next five chapters, we analyze the **selection environment**: the underlying architecture that determines which claims spread, which stabilize, and which disappear. Rather than focusing on individual intent, this section examines the pressures that act on information as it moves through modern systems.

Chapter 9 (Attention Markets) examines time scarcity. It shows why arousal, certainty, and novelty are not merely tactics, but adaptive responses in crowded environments.

Chapter 10 (Algorithmic Distribution) analyzes machine-mediated routing. It shows how optimization for engagement creates feedback loops that reward conflict and penalize nuance.

Chapter 11 (Context Collapse) explores the effects of mixed and adversarial audiences. It explains why speech becomes defensive and simplified when speakers cannot predict who is listening.

Chapter 12 (Governance) looks at rule-setting under scale. It shows how moderation systems flatten ambiguity into binary categories in order to function at volume.

Chapter 13 (Ecosystem Dynamics) integrates these forces. It shows how attention, algorithms, context, and governance align to form a **drift pipeline**—a structural process that moves claims from loose explanations into hardened identities.

By the end of this section, drift should no longer appear accidental. It is the equilibrium outcome of systems optimized for speed, scale, and engagement. Understanding that environment is a prerequisite for intervention. If the output is distorted, the machine producing it must be examined first.

CHAPTER 9

Attention Markets: Arousal, Certainty, Novelty

Modern knowledge now moves through an **attention market**.[3]

The defining scarcity in this market is notice. Claims compete continuously for limited perceptual bandwidth, and selection increasingly operates on the ability to capture attention long enough to be processed and passed along. In this environment, performance characteristics shape which claims circulate widely and which remain confined.

Three dimensions dominate selection: salience, speed, and repeatability.

Salience governs capture. Claims that evoke arousal—alarm, outrage, hope, or fear—interrupt the stream and command focus. Speed governs payoff. Claims that land quickly outperform those that require setup, context, or patience. Repeatability governs friction. Claims that can be restated cleanly and consistently travel farther than those that depend on careful phrasing.

These pressures shape more than style. They function as a filter that moves claims forward through the drift pipeline.

One pressure is arousal advantage. Content framed around urgency or threat spreads rapidly. Emotional intensity shortens the interval between exposure and sharing. This dynamic applies broadly: accurate claims framed with heightened urgency often outperform calmer formulations.

Another pressure is certainty advantage. In attention markets, confidence operates as a proxy for credibility. It lowers evaluation cost for audiences deciding what to accept and share. As a result,

---

3   Tim Wu, *The Attention Merchants: The Epic Scramble to Get Inside Our Heads* (New York: Knopf, 2016), especially Part V (on clickbait, microfame incentives, and competitive attention markets).

language that projects certainty circulates more easily than language that preserves ambiguity. Over time, qualifiers fall away because they raise cognitive cost.

A third pressure is novelty advantage. Attention systems reward what appears new, counterintuitive, or surprising. Sharp reframings of familiar issues often outperform careful restatements of established knowledge. Across repeated cycles, this pushes claims toward increasingly distinctive interpretations.

A fourth pressure is narrative advantage. Stories travel more effectively than models. Claims embedded in clear arcs—conflict, resolution, moral alignment—are easier to remember and transmit than claims grounded in statistical or systemic explanation. Moral clarity offers an efficient cognitive path; causal complexity demands sustained effort.

Together, these pressures account for the force of the transition from Stage 1 to Stage 2. When a claim leaves a serious tradition, it encounters the attention market as a new environment. To move through it, the claim adapts. Caveats, methods, and contextual limits fall away because they increase friction, not because they lack validity.

The same pressures explain movement from Stage 2 to Stage 3. Once a meme extract circulates widely, the environment rewards those who can assemble fragments into a complete explanatory story. The prompt shifts from *"What's the takeaway?"* to *"What's really going on?"* Folk theories that provide closure circulate more effectively than provisional accounts that retain uncertainty.

The resulting patterns are consistent. Qualifier stripping becomes routine, and audiences adjust expectations accordingly. Moral framing becomes prominent, because moral conflict attracts attention more reliably than technical disagreement. Correction slows as claims lengthen and intensify, while careful updates require time and sustained focus.

The mechanism here is structural. These outcomes arise from competition acting on form. As attention becomes the primary currency, the environment selects for claims optimized to capture and hold it. Drift follows as a consequence of adaptation.

This sets the conditions for the next layer of pressure. Attention markets influence what people choose to share. Algorithmic distribution determines what is routed, amplified, and stabilized at scale.

CHAPTER 10

Algorithmic Distribution: Optimization as Epistemology

Once claims enter large-scale circulation, selection no longer operates primarily through individual attention.

Algorithmic distribution governs what is routed, amplified, and sustained at scale. Together, these layers form a selection system. Human behavior generates signals; algorithms determine which signals persist.

The governing logic of this layer is optimization. Claims are evaluated continuously against engagement metrics, and those that perform well gain extended visibility. Over time, this process shapes what becomes familiar, repeated, and stable within public circulation.

The pressure operating here is functional. Algorithmic systems respond to measurable interaction—clicks, comments, watch time, repeat viewing. Formats that generate consistent signals are reinforced. Formats that produce weaker signals receive less exposure as routing shifts elsewhere.[4]

This environment favors format fit. Certain structures generate clear, interpretable signals: emotionally legible narratives, recurring frames, identifiable antagonists, and claims that can be consumed quickly and independently. Other structures demand more from the audience. Nuance diffuses response. Context-heavy explanations slow consumption. Claims that invite uncertainty generate less immediate interaction. Over time, these forms lose visibility as circulation concentrates around lower-friction alternatives.

The result is a compounding dynamic often described as selection amplification.

---

4   Safiya Umoja Noble, *Algorithms of Oppression: How Search Engines Reinforce Racism* (New York: NYU Press, 2018), Introduction and early chapters on ranking incentives and the non-neutrality of retrieval systems.

Small performance differences accumulate. When one version of a claim elicits slightly more interaction than another, it receives greater exposure. That exposure produces additional interaction data, which reinforces the preference and extends the gap further. Repetition turns marginal advantages into durable visibility. One version becomes familiar, then dominant, then taken as representative of the conversation simply through repeated exposure.

This dynamic explains why algorithmic systems consistently elevate drift-shaped objects.

Early in circulation, compressed forms characteristic of Stage 2 gain traction. Headlines, clips, and simplified claims generate fast, legible signals. As engagement deepens, more totalizing explanations characteristic of Stage 3 gain advantage. Unified narratives sustain attention longer than provisional heuristics. At later stages, conflict-oriented material associated with Stage 4 performs reliably. Moralized disagreement sustains recursive interaction: responses to responses, reinterpretations, and public escalation.

Across stages, the pattern remains stable. Algorithmic selection favors forms that are easy to evaluate, amplify, and stabilize.[5]

Several downstream effects follow.

Visibility concentrates around a limited number of frames as attention accumulates. Repetition creates an impression of consensus as familiar shapes dominate circulation. Over time, claims sharpen to maintain engagement, reinforcing certainty and reducing tolerance for ambiguity.

Within this environment, drift emerges as the stable outcome of repeated selection rather than as an exception. Claims that survive are those that adapt to the pressures imposed by routing, amplification, and scale.

These dynamics prepare the next pressure layer. As claims reach larger and more heterogeneous audiences, the contexts they were

---

5   Noble, *Algorithms of Oppression*.

built within collapse. Scale produces mixed audiences. Mixed audiences reshape how people speak.

That pressure is examined in the next chapter.

CHAPTER 11

Context Collapse: Adversarial Audiences and Defensive Speech

So far, this section has examined attention markets and algorithmic distribution. A third pressure shapes how claims are expressed, operating at a more personal level: the presence of adversarial audiences.

Context collapse occurs when distinct audiences—friends, colleagues, supervisors, critics, and strangers—converge into a single field of visibility. Speech that was once shaped for a specific setting is now produced under conditions of broad and persistent exposure.

This exposure alters how speakers adapt.

When audience boundaries blur, speakers respond by making their positions unmistakable. Language shifts toward clarity of stance. Ambiguity carries cost. Nuance invites interpretation. Over time, a contextual speaker gives way to a public-facing one. Communication orients less toward mutual understanding and more toward durability under scrutiny.

At an operational level, this changes what language is optimized for. Expression is shaped with an eye toward the most consequential possible audience—the listener whose interpretation carries the greatest potential impact if encountered later, outside its original context. The presence of that listener is not required. Anticipation alone is enough to shape speech.[6]

Under these conditions, communication adapts through a small set of recurring mechanics.

One is pre-emptive signaling. Phrases such as "to be clear" or

---

6   Danah Boyd, *It's Complicated: The Social Lives of Networked Teens* (New Haven: Yale University Press, 2014), chapters on networked publics, privacy, and context collapse.

"let me say this upfront" function as boundary-setting devices. They narrow the range of plausible interpretations and establish alignment early.

Another is over-commitment. Speakers gravitate toward stronger formulations than their private beliefs might warrant, because decisive language reads as stable and reliable. Certainty acquires protective value.

A third is simplification. Caveats and conditional phrasing increase interpretive surface area. To reduce exposure, complexity is streamlined. This is less about persuasion than about risk management.

Together, these adaptations help explain the transition from Stage 3 to Stage 4.

In mixed audiences, explanation alone no longer suffices. Folk theories circulate under continuous visibility, where even silence communicates position. Taking a stance becomes legible action. The guiding question shifts from "Is this explanation adequate?" to "What does endorsing this communicate about me?"

The downstream effects follow a consistent pattern.

- Interpretation centers on alignment rather than meaning.

- Revision acquires visibility costs, as changes in position leave durable records.

- Attention moves from evaluating claims to inferring affiliation.

The mechanism at work here is exposure. When speech takes place under conditions of persistent visibility and anticipated hostility, claims are shaped increasingly by the need to withstand scrutiny and less by the goal of representing the world in full detail.

This pressure feeds directly into the next layer of the system. As audiences become more adversarial, enforceability rises in importance. Norms formalize. Boundaries sharpen. Governance shifts toward rule-setting and control.

That transition is the focus of the next chapter.

At this point, circulation alone is no longer sufficient; sustained coordination at scale requires formalization, and claims begin to encounter institutions.

CHAPTER 12

Governance and Moderation: Enforceability Becomes Reality

So far, this book has examined attention markets, algorithmic routing, and context collapse. The final environmental pressure is governance.

Governance emerges wherever speech must be moderated, rules must be enforced, and ambiguity must be managed across large, heterogeneous populations. While attention markets organize around visibility, governance systems organize around enforceability.

Scale defines this environment. When millions of people interact in a shared space, informal norms lose reliability. Shared background assumptions thin out, interpretive context fragments, and a stable sense of "we" becomes difficult to sustain. In response, systems shift toward explicit rules, identifiable violations, and defensible enforcement procedures.

This produces a selection environment that favors legibility.

At scale, claims must fit into recognizable categories. Governance systems operate through distinctions such as allowed and disallowed, safe and unsafe, harassment and debate, misinformation and satire. These categories make enforcement possible across diverse contexts and at high volume.

Context-dependent expression carries higher evaluation costs. Assessing irony, layered meaning, or shared cultural reference requires reconstructing intent, history, and tone—work that is difficult for human moderators and infeasible for automated systems at scale. As a result, speech that maps cleanly onto categorical definitions travels more easily through governance filters.

Speakers adapt to these conditions. To persist under enforcement, claims are expressed in forms that rulebooks and machines can reliably interpret. Ambiguity recedes. Language aligns more tightly with sanctioned positions. Explicit moral framing becomes common, not as a matter of philosophical refinement, but because it clarifies intent and lowers interpretive burden. Moral clarity reads as legible.

These pressures accelerate the transition from Stage 4 to Stage 5.

When enforcement relies on categorical distinctions, people reorganize around those distinctions. Beliefs take on the function of identity markers. Labels such as safe or unsafe transform positions into high-stakes signals. Governance shapes more than what circulates; it reshapes how belief is socially organized.

This environment produces predictable adaptations.

One adaptation is the euphemism treadmill. As explicit language becomes regulated, meaning migrates into coded forms—symbols, inside jokes, indirect references—that preserve signaling while maintaining plausible deniability.

Another adaptation is platform migration. Claims move into less regulated spaces, where they intensify under fewer constraints, and later reenter mainstream environments in more consolidated forms.

A third adaptation is procedural reframing. Assertions are presented as questions, hypotheticals, or commentary in order to navigate the boundary between rule definitions and enforcement thresholds.

These adaptations generate characteristic failure modes.

Sanctioned content can acquire symbolic weight, turning restriction into a source of meaning and cohesion. Enforcement actions are sometimes read as epistemic signals rather than procedural decisions, reshaping how truth and authority are inferred. Communities may organize around shared prohibitions, with boundaries defined by what cannot be said rather than what is affirmed.

Governance operates as a necessary condition for large-scale coordination. Any system operating at scale depends on rules to sustain participation. At the same time, governance introduces selection pressures. It favors claims that are simple, categorical, and legible. It elevates expressions that can be clearly identified, enforced, and defended across institutional, adversarial, and automated contexts.[7]

At this point, the full selection environment comes into view. Attention shapes what attracts notice. Algorithms determine what is amplified. Context collapse shapes how people speak. Governance determines what persists.

Together, these pressures do more than alter information flow. They shape the forms of belief that stabilize in public life.

---

7   Tarleton Gillespie, *Custodians of the Internet: Platforms, Content Moderation, and the Hidden Decisions That Shape Social Media* (New Haven: Yale University Press, 2018), chapters on moderation as constitutive governance and enforceability at scale.

CHAPTER 13

Ecosystem Dynamics: From Drift to Pipeline

At sufficient scale, selection pressures begin to interact.

Earlier chapters examined individual pressures in isolation: how attention rewards arousal, how algorithms amplify engagement, how mixed audiences shape expression, and how governance enforces legibility. In practice, claims encounter these forces together. They move through ecosystems—interconnected networks of creators, platforms, communities, and distribution channels that reinforce one another.

At this scale, drift takes on a patterned form. Claim movement becomes structured routing.

The defining feature of an ecosystem is multi-node reinforcement. A claim appears in one format, is reframed in another, amplified in a third, and normalized in a fourth. A tweet becomes a podcast segment, which becomes a newsletter essay, which becomes a group-chat assumption. Each node applies its own local incentives, and the cumulative effect is convergence. Repeated exposure across formats and sources transforms an interpretation into a felt baseline.

At this point, drift organizes into a **pipeline**.

A pipeline emerges through alignment. The system begins to move claims through a familiar sequence of transformations, producing consistent outputs across contexts.[8]

The process begins with seeding. Large volumes of Stage 2 extracts—clips, headlines, slogans—enter circulation. Most fade

---

8   Yochai Benkler, Robert Faris, and Hal Roberts, *Network Propaganda: Manipulation, Disinformation, and Radicalization in American Politics* (New York: Oxford University Press, 2018), chapters on propaganda feedback loops, ecosystem asymmetries, and pipeline dynamics.

quickly. A small subset resonates and persists. These are copied, remixed, and reinforced as they move through the ecosystem.

As extracts cluster, theorizing follows. Stage 3 folk theories form to connect fragments into an explanatory frame. The ecosystem increasingly rewards those who can integrate new events into the emerging story. Audiences shift from seeking isolated signals to seeking accounts that organize signals into coherence.

As the theory stabilizes, sorting dynamics take hold. Stage 4 pressures dominate. Fluency with the framework signals competence. Interpretive contests emerge around emphasis, threat identification, and boundary definition. The claim's value increasingly lies in its capacity to rank participants.

Over time, the pipeline reaches hardening. Stage 5 identity systems consolidate to stabilize the group. The ecosystem now functions as a boundary-maintenance system. Claims persist because they anchor belonging and alignment.

At this stage, ecosystems become susceptible to capture.

Capture arises through incentive alignment. One form is ideological capture, where a belief system shifts from interpretive lens to membership marker. Coherence and alignment take priority, and dissent is treated as destabilizing.

Another form is commercial capture. Retention dynamics favor intensity, certainty, and affective escalation. Content that sustains attention sharpens boundaries and reinforces dependence loops. Individual actors may act sincerely, while the system consistently selects versions of their output that maximize engagement.

This reframes how propaganda emerges.

Rather than entering from outside, propaganda often crystallizes within an ecosystem that is already shaped to reward it. It appears once the system reliably favors simplicity, certainty, cohesion, and clear adversaries.

These traits align with the pressures produced by attention

markets, algorithmic optimization, context collapse, and large-scale governance. When an ecosystem consistently rewards these properties, it develops a structural vacancy that propaganda readily occupies. The specific message varies; the shape remains stable.

Pipeline dynamics produce recognizable signals.

- Uniformity appears as independent voices converge on shared metaphors and framings.

- Boundary sensitivity increases as partial agreement becomes a test of alignment.

- Scandal cycles accelerate as periodic outrage renews cohesion without resolving underlying questions.

These patterns reflect system behavior. They arise from environments operating according to their incentive structures.

The model describes how claims move under pressure. The chapters that follow trace that movement end-to-end across real domains, focusing on structure and function rather than adjudicating final belief.

Case Studies: How to Read What Follows

The Drift Model makes a strong claim: under stable selection pressures, claims change in predictable ways. Similar transition patterns recur across domains that otherwise share little in common. Part IV demonstrates that predictability in practice.

The posture of these case studies is intentionally restrained. They are mechanism-first and observational. Each case traces how a claim bundle changes as it moves across environments—how constraints fall away, how new elements accumulate, how revision grows costly, and how correction pathways narrow over time.

In this book, a case functions as a diagnostic instrument. It follows a bounded origin claim, the extraction that increased its portability, the folk theory that consolidated it, the status dynamics that made it performable, and the identity mechanisms that raised the cost of exit. The emphasis remains on tracing movement rather than cataloging every historical detail.

These cases focus on constraint degradation rather than belief assessment. Even when an origin claim proves inaccurate, the central question concerns how its structure changed during transmission and which selection pressures shaped that change.

Throughout this section, attention remains on transformation under pressure. The analytical task is to observe how claims evolve as they travel, and how predictable pressures shape that evolution.

CHAPTER 14

Case Study Template: The Forensic Audit

With the theory in place, the book now turns to application.

Part IV presents a series of forensic audits. Each case study follows a shared structure so that analyses remain comparable across domains and focused on mechanism rather than judgment. The purpose of an audit is to trace how a claim changed function as it moved through public circulation, and how pressure reshaped its constraints over time.

Every case opens with a **Case Card**. This provides a compact structural overview before the narrative begins, allowing the reader to see the relevant dynamics at a glance.

The Case Card tracks four variables:

- **Domain** — The field in which the claim originated (such as health, politics, or technology), establishing baseline norms for evidence and correction.

- **Origin Bundle** — The reconstructed Stage 1 claim, including scope conditions, supporting substrate, and falsifiers.

- **Dominant Pressures** — The selection forces shaping transmission at the relevant moment, such as attention, algorithmic routing, or governance constraints.

- **Lock-In Point** — The stage at which revision became socially or institutionally costly enough to resist correction.

With this structure in place, the audit proceeds through a consistent sequence.

Step 1: The Origin Claim (Stage 1 — Bounded)

Each audit begins by reconstructing the claim as it functioned within a serious tradition. This establishes a baseline. The focus is on identifying the version that carried explicit constraints: where the claim applied, what evidence supported it, and what conditions would have required revision.

This reconstruction anchors the rest of the analysis. It allows later changes to be evaluated as transformations of a bounded proposition rather than as isolated slogans.

Step 2: The Extraction Delta (Stage 2)

The audit then identifies the moment the claim became portable. This usually involves a specific artifact—a headline, clip, post, or summary—that enabled rapid transmission across contexts.

Attention shifts to the trade-offs introduced at this point. Which constraints fell away? Which elements were amplified? Qualifiers, scope limits, and uncertainty often recede, while certainty, urgency, or moral framing become more prominent. The question here concerns exchange: how much constraint fidelity was traded for speed and reach.

Step 3: Folk Theory Consolidation (Stage 3)

Next, the analysis traces how extracts combined into a shared explanation. At this stage, the claim answers a broader question for a community: *"What is going on?"*

The audit follows how scope expands, how monocausal narratives form, and how evidence is recruited to support the emerging story. Confirming examples gain prominence, anomalies lose salience, and the theory becomes the default interpretive frame.

STEP 4: STATUS SORTING (STAGE 4)

The focus then shifts to social function.

At this stage, the claim operates as a sorting mechanism. The audit examines how fluency with the framework signals competence and how alignment affects rank. Insider language, approved framings, and recognizable shibboleths mark belonging.

The reward structure becomes visible here. Speed, certainty, and performative confidence often receive more reinforcement than calibration. When revision carries a status penalty, the claim has begun to function as a ranking instrument.

STEP 5: IDENTITY LOCK-IN (STAGE 5)

The final stage assesses whether the system has stabilized as identity.

The audit identifies moral boundaries—who is inside and who is outside—and notes which questions can be raised safely and which carry risk. Central to this stage is exit cost: what follows when someone revises or leaves the belief system. When revision entails significant social loss, the system has locked.

STEP 6: INTERVENTION WINDOWS

Each audit concludes with a structural postmortem. Rather than offering prescriptions, the analysis identifies **intervention windows**: points at which alternative design choices, norms, or incentives might have reduced drift or lowered the cost of remaining accurate.

The guiding question is where accuracy could have been made easier to sustain, rather than where enforcement could have been intensified.

ANALYTICAL INTEGRITY: WHAT MAKES A CASE VIABLE

For a case study to function as a forensic audit, several conditions must be met.

A viable case includes a clearly reconstructed origin bundle, a concrete extraction artifact, and evidence that the claim later functioned as a social sorting mechanism. The analysis remains descriptive rather than advocative, tracing transformations rather than adjudicating positions.

These conditions ensure that Part IV remains focused on mechanics. The cases illuminate how claims lose constraints and how information gradually takes on social weight—step by step, under pressure.

CHAPTER 15

Health & Wellness Pipelines

WHY HEALTH CLAIMS DRIFT SO FAST

In high-stakes domains, drift becomes embodied.

Health and wellness claims move through the drift pipeline faster than almost any other category because they sit at the intersection of anxiety and agency. Physical vulnerability sharpens the demand for explanation and action. When the body feels unreliable, uncertainty becomes difficult to carry. People want to know why they are tired, why they are sick, and what specific intervention might restore equilibrium.

At the point of origin, medical science offers a different kind of answer. Inside serious traditions, health claims are probabilistic. They describe risk factors, partial correlations, and mechanisms that often remain unresolved. Etiology is complex, and precision frequently trades off with immediate clarity.

As claims move into the wellness ecosystem, the trade-off reverses. Ambiguity is reframed as a design problem. The body is treated as a system of inputs and outputs. Protocols take the place of probabilities. What resists full explanation is translated into action.

This chapter follows how a bounded biological claim moves through that pipeline—and how, over time, it organizes identity.

DRIFT ACCELERANTS IN THIS DOMAIN

Health claims drift quickly because of a distinctive environmental mix.

The evidence base is often statistical rather than binary. Epidemiology and systems biology produce distributions, associations, and ranges rather than simple thresholds. This leaves interpretive space that invites more definitive framing. Health is also culturally linked to choice, which encourages explanations that emphasize discipline, knowledge, or purity.

Subjective experience carries unusual authority. Bodily sensation provides immediate feedback, and once a feeling is named and explained, it acquires explanatory weight. Measurement gaps are frequently interpreted as limitations of existing tools rather than as expressions of uncertainty.

Wellness claims also compress efficiently. Phrases such as "the root cause," "one lever," or "one weird trick," paired with before-and-after visuals, deliver rapid validation at low cognitive cost.

Many participants enter these pipelines after experiences of institutional ambiguity. Persistent symptoms alongside normal laboratory results create frustration. The pipeline supplies validation where medicine offered probabilistic restraint. Together, these conditions accelerate drift.

THE ORIGIN CLAIM

One illustrative case is the contemporary "cortisol control" pipeline.

The origin claim arises in neuroendocrinology. Cortisol is a glucocorticoid hormone released by the adrenal glands to mobilize energy in response to waking and stress. It follows a diurnal rhythm. Acute elevations support adaptation. Chronically elevated baseline levels are associated with increased metabolic, inflammatory, and cardiovascular risk.

Several constraints accompany this claim. Cortisol is essential for survival, and deficient levels are life-threatening. The concept of "adrenal fatigue," framed as stress-induced adrenal failure, does not appear in formal diagnostic systems. The underlying phenomenon—HPA-axis dysregulation—varies widely across individuals and contexts and resists reduction to a single metric.

Within serious traditions, this bundle travels intact. Scope, substrate, and falsifiers remain attached. The objective is regulation within range rather than elimination.

Extraction Under Attention

As the claim enters the attention market, its function shifts.

Adaptive roles recede, and the hormone is recast as an antagonist. Short-form content diagnoses "cortisol face." Advertisements rename it "the belly-fat hormone." Visual cues stand in for laboratory measures. A broad set of common discomforts—fatigue, bloating, anxiety—are unified under a single explanatory label.

Rhythm drops out of the frame. Necessity fades. Distinctions between acute and chronic activation lose prominence. What remains is a generalized threat.

A probabilistic relationship between stress and inflammation condenses into a binary diagnostic. Puffiness maps to cortisol. Stress maps to damage.

When the Extract Becomes an Explanation

As extracts circulate, they assemble into a shared narrative.

A folk theory forms around "dysregulation." Modern life is portrayed as a continuous stressor that keeps the body in permanent fight-or-flight. Phones, emails, processed food, artificial light—each becomes part of a single explanatory field. Weight gain, anxiety, burnout, and brain fog align as downstream effects of an invisible driver.

Scope expands. Cortisol shifts from a lab value to a felt state. Wiredness, fatigue, and insomnia all fit comfortably within the frame.

Evidence begins to function as reinforcement rather than

constraint. Stressful moments are incorporated as confirmation. The absence of clear measurement becomes an argument for deeper, more personalized dysfunction.

WHEN FLUENCY BECOMES STATUS

At this point, the framework takes on a social role.

"Regulation" becomes a marker of competence. Morning routines are documented. Alarm clocks are removed. Sunlight is recorded. Mineral blends and supplements are displayed. Heart-rate variability screenshots serve as visible alignment.

A shared vocabulary develops: "nervous system regulation," "healing the HPA axis," "bioavailable," "soft era." Fluency signals sophistication. Deviation invites reinterpretation.

High performers who disregard the protocol are recast as hormonally burdened. Coffee on an empty stomach becomes diagnostic. Stress tolerance itself acquires symbolic meaning.

THE MORAL BOUNDARY

The final transition occurs when the protocol organizes moral space.

The landscape divides into contrasting categories: regulated and inflamed, natural and captured, functional wellness and conventional medicine. Clinicians who reference normal laboratory results are recast as dismissive. Studies that fail to replicate the narrative are set aside as insufficiently sensitive to "functional burnout" or "bio-individuality."

Exit costs rise. Leaving the protocol is reframed as neglect. Fatigue shifts from a common human experience to an evaluative signal. Explanations once attributed to workload, chance, or aging are reinterpreted as personal failure.

The system stabilizes.

WHY THIS DOMAIN LOCKS IN

Health pipelines harden quickly because several reinforcing mechanisms converge.

Anecdote carries exceptional weight. A single lived experience is emotionally legible and personally authoritative. Protocols are embodied as rituals, turning belief into daily practice and raising the cost of revision. Unified explanations promise relief from fragmentation, offering a single cause where medicine presents multiple interacting factors.

The clarity of "one cause" sustains commitment long after its explanatory reach has narrowed.

WHERE DRIFT COULD HAVE BEEN SLOWED

Auditing cases like this highlights points of leverage.

Earlier in the pipeline, modest design choices could have preserved constraint fidelity: visualizations of cortisol's U-shaped risk curve; narrative distinctions between acute and chronic stress; respected voices acknowledging unexplained variance and mixed outcomes even under disciplined behavior.

Each intervention lowers the cost of remaining accurate. Each reduces pressure toward identity formation.

Once bodily experience becomes a moral signal, evidence alone carries limited force. Correction must engage not only belief, but belonging.

CHAPTER 16

Psychology & Therapy Pipelines

WHY PSYCHOLOGY CLAIMS DRIFT

If health claims drift through anxiety, psychology claims drift through pain.

In this domain, the raw material is human behavior rather than physiology. The boundaries are interpretive by nature. Concepts such as a "toxic relationship" or "emotional abuse" draw meaning from language, memory, context, and perspective. Because these categories lack hard physical markers, they invite expansion. Terms designed to describe specific clinical patterns often extend outward, gradually encompassing broader forms of discomfort, conflict, and harm.

As a result, psychology is especially susceptible to concept expansion: the movement of harm-related concepts from narrow clinical contexts into wider moral use.

In this domain, the drift pipeline functions as a pain-translation system. It takes the ambiguity of interpersonal conflict and renders it legible through categories, scripts, and roles. A painful breakup becomes a recognizable cycle. A difficult boss acquires a diagnostic label. Confusion resolves into explanation, and emotional ambiguity organizes into named patterns.

This chapter traces how clinical tools intended to support self-understanding evolve into social instruments used to identify adversaries.

DRIFT ACCELERANTS IN THIS DOMAIN

Psychology pipelines accelerate under a distinctive set of pressures.

Many psychological concepts begin as descriptive models—
ways of naming recurring patterns without assigning moral
judgment. As these concepts travel, description gradually takes
on prescriptive force. "Avoidant attachment" comes to signify a
warning category. "Dysregulation" becomes a verdict rather than a
state.

These concepts also carry high identity relevance. Psychological
frameworks do more than describe behavior; they provide
narratives about who people are, why suffering occurs, and how
relationships unravel. This makes them especially potent material
for identity formation.

There is also a strong demand for explanatory closure. Pain resists
partial accounts. Simple relational explanations feel insufficient,
while diagnostic narratives offer comprehensive meaning.
Ambiguity resolves when responsibility is localized and the cause
is made legible.

Finally, the attention economy rewards distance diagnosis.
Content creators gain visibility by analyzing strangers—former
partners, public figures, celebrities—using limited artifacts such as
clips, anecdotes, or screenshots. Diagnostic authority expands as
direct assessment fades from view.

Together, these pressures accelerate drift.

THE ORIGIN CLAIM

A clear illustration is the contemporary "narcissism" pipeline.

The origin claim emerges from clinical psychology. Narcissistic
Personality Disorder is defined as a pervasive pattern of
grandiosity, need for admiration, and diminished empathy
that produces significant functional impairment. It affects a
small proportion of the population and requires careful clinical
evaluation over time. Narcissism exists along a spectrum, with the
disorder representing a specific and severe configuration.

Several constraints accompany this claim. Traits associated

with narcissism overlap with insecurity, trauma responses, and situational stress. Ethical standards restrict diagnosis to cases involving direct evaluation. Treatment is challenging, and outcomes vary, but the condition affects patients as well as those around them.

Within serious traditions, this bundle travels with its weight intact. Scope, substrate, and falsifiers remain attached.

EXTRACTION UNDER ATTENTION

As the claim enters wider circulation, its function shifts.

Clinical boundaries loosen as the concept is repackaged as a relational diagnostic tool. Short videos promise rapid identification. Visual summaries outline recognizable patterns. Disorientation itself becomes interpretable evidence, offering clarity through classification.

Rarity recedes from view. Functional impairment becomes secondary. Distinctions between trait and disorder lose salience. The concept condenses into a recognizable antagonist.

Attention moves from internal pathology to personal experience. The explanatory frame shifts from clinical assessment to relational narrative.

WHEN THE EXTRACT BECOMES AN EXPLANATION

As extracts circulate, they consolidate into a shared story.

A folk theory forms around the "narcissistic abuse cycle." Relationships follow a recognizable arc: idealization, devaluation, discard. Roles solidify. One party acquires interior complexity; the other becomes legible through predictable patterns.

The framework expands to accommodate all observed behavior. Generosity signals manipulation. Distance signals punishment.

Apologies fit established scripts. Disagreement aligns with expectation.

Alternative explanations lose traction. Ordinary conflict becomes diagnostic material. The theory functions as a complete interpretive system.

At this stage, evidence reinforces rather than constrains. The framework explains behavior and incorporates disagreement as confirmation of its own reach.

When Fluency Becomes Status

The pipeline then acquires a social dimension.

Fluency in therapeutic language signals competence. Familiarity with terms such as "flying monkeys," "gray rock," or "DARVO" marks participation and experience. Diagnosis becomes performative, enacted through commentary on public figures or mediated relationships.

Interpretive certainty gains value. Hesitation invites reinterpretation. Vigilance aligns with credibility.

The framework now functions as a status engine.

The Moral Boundary

The final transition occurs when the framework organizes identity.

Social space resolves into distinct categories: survivors and abusers, Empaths and Narcs. Behavioral strategies such as no-contact become moral reference points. Attempts at mutual understanding are reframed through the established lens.

The system stabilizes through internal consistency. Diagnostic terms double as protective tools, filtering feedback and maintaining coherence. Identity alignment shapes interpretation.

Exit costs increase. Revising the narrative carries social risk, including loss of community or reclassification within the framework. Persistence reflects social stability as much as explanatory power.

DISTINCTIVE FAILURE MODES

Psychology pipelines exhibit characteristic distortions.

Abstract constructs acquire concrete form. Models are treated as entities. Diagnostic categories take on personal identity.

Scope expands as language stretches to cover everyday conflict. Precision thins where discernment matters most.

Falsifiers lose influence. The framework accommodates divergent outcomes within a single explanation, reinforcing internal coherence.

Therapeutic language takes on strategic use. Concepts such as "boundaries" and "safety" organize expectations and preferences, shaping interaction norms.

WHERE DRIFT COULD HAVE BEEN SLOWED

As with health pipelines, auditing these cases highlights leverage points.

Constraint fidelity could have been preserved through stronger norms emphasizing behavior over identity—describing actions and patterns without essentializing people. Framing relational harm as dynamic rather than archetypal supports accountability while maintaining agency.

Clear limits on distance diagnosis would have anchored clinical tools within appropriate contexts, reducing incentives for speculative labeling.

Once pain becomes a foundation for identity, evidence alone carries limited leverage. Correction must engage social belonging as well as belief.

CHAPTER 17

Politics & Moral Psychology Pipelines

WHY POLITICAL CLAIMS DRIFT

If health is where anxiety is processed, and psychology is where pain is interpreted, politics is where fear and power are organized.

This domain concentrates nearly every pressure described so far. Context collapses completely. Algorithmic amplification operates continuously. Identity stakes rise to their highest level. Political claims are produced under surveillance, routed through engagement-optimizing systems, and read as signals of moral alignment. In this environment, belief and identity draw close together.

Claims about policy or political philosophy therefore change function quickly. As they circulate, they acquire a new role as permission structures—frameworks that organize exclusion, justify coercive action, or authorize moral aggression. Concepts originally developed to protect democratic systems are especially susceptible to this transformation. Once separated from their historical and institutional context, they often reorganize around new uses.

This chapter follows one such transformation.

DRIFT ACCELERANTS IN THIS DOMAIN

Political pipelines consolidate rapidly because of a distinctive configuration of pressures.

Political beliefs draw clear boundaries between groups. Alignment communicates membership, while disagreement signals distance. Positions are frequently read as indicators of character, intent, or threat.

Political speech also travels across multiple audiences simultaneously. Statements function less as persuasion and more as performance—signaling loyalty to allies while marking opposition to adversaries. Algorithms reinforce this pattern by amplifying clarity of alignment, confidence, and intensity.

Norms evolve quickly in this environment. Expectations shift, and the social cost of lagging behind those shifts becomes salient. Exclusion operates as a real mechanism, shaping participation and accelerating drift.

THE ORIGIN CLAIM

A canonical example is the contemporary "Paradox of Tolerance" pipeline.

The claim originates in political philosophy, in Karl Popper's *The Open Society and Its Enemies* (1945). Popper addressed a specific historical problem: how a liberal democracy can sustain itself in the presence of movements that use democratic freedoms to dismantle democratic institutions.

His argument was conditional and bounded. Unlimited tolerance, Popper argued, could undermine tolerance if a society failed to respond to movements that rejected rational argument and relied on violence or deception. Even in such cases, he emphasized proportionality. Suppression appeared as a last-resort response, applicable only when argument and institutional process had broken down.

The scope of the claim was narrow. It applied to violent, insurrectionary movements rather than to ordinary political disagreement. Within serious traditions, this bundle traveled with its context intact: postwar Europe, fascism, and the historical collapse of democratic institutions under force.

EXTRACTION UNDER ATTENTION

As the claim enters mass circulation, its form changes.

The argument compresses into a visual binary. A common artifact depicts a tolerant society welcoming an intolerant figure, who then destroys it from within. This format privileges immediacy and recognizability. Nuanced conditions—such as proportionality, last resort, and the availability of argument—fade from view. What remains is a compact directive: *No tolerance for the intolerant.*

Scope narrows and then expands in a different direction. "Intolerance" becomes a flexible category, open to substitution. The concept shifts from an emergency brake into a standing authorization that can be applied across a wide range of disagreements.

WHEN THE EXTRACT BECOMES AN EXPLANATION

As these extracts circulate, they consolidate into a shared explanatory frame.

Tolerance is recast as a peace treaty. Certain expressions are interpreted as violations that dissolve procedural protections. Debate is reframed as a sign of naivety. Suppressive responses appear as expressions of democratic commitment rather than departures from it.

The framework broadens quickly. Minor infractions—voting preferences, imprecise language, resistance to evolving terminology—are incorporated as evidence that argument has exhausted its utility. Isolated cases of extremist violence or hate speech come to stand in for systemic failure, extending the logic of emergency to routine conditions.

WHEN AGGRESSION BECOMES STATUS

At this point, the claim acquires a social function.

Public expressions of aggression signal resolve and moral seriousness. Calls for exclusion, de-platforming, or coercive measures circulate as markers of clarity. Familiar slogans operate as shibboleths, identifying alignment and commitment.

The center of gravity shifts from defending democratic procedures to demonstrating readiness to confront perceived threats. Confidence and decisiveness carry social rewards. Procedural liberalism recedes as a valued orientation, while confrontation gains symbolic weight.

The claim now operates as a status engine.

THE MORAL BOUNDARY

The final transition occurs when the framework organizes identity.

Political space divides into categorical roles. Defending the procedural rights of an opponent is interpreted as affiliation. Proximity acquires meaning. Metaphors such as the "table of Nazis" function as boundary-closing devices, equating association with endorsement.

At this stage, the framework stabilizes through self-reinforcement. Appeals to free speech are interpreted through the lens of harm prevention. Calls for debate register as signals of bad faith. Revision carries substantial social cost, and alternatives to suppression appear increasingly distant.

Persistence follows from structure rather than argument. Leaving the framework entails risk to standing, relationships, and moral identity.

DISTINCTIVE FAILURE MODES

Political pipelines display several characteristic dynamics.

Political speech is performed under adversarial visibility, encouraging defensive certainty and overcommitment. Coalition maintenance exerts continuous pressure, bundling positions and raising the cost of dissent. Moral language provides high legibility, traveling faster and farther than technical arguments about trade-offs. Algorithms amplify this asymmetry, favoring emotionally charged accusation over procedural detail.

Governance actions also acquire symbolic meaning. Content restrictions or platform interventions are read as epistemic signals, transforming moderation into perceived adjudication.

WHERE DRIFT COULD HAVE BEEN SLOWED

As with other domains, auditing this pipeline reveals points of leverage.

Constraint fidelity could be supported by restoring the emergency context of Popper's argument, including its emphasis on proportionality and last resort. Emphasizing procedures over positions would redirect disputes toward system design rather than moral worthiness. Framing dissent as strategic disagreement rather than disloyalty would expand the space for revision.

When politics functions as identity infrastructure, argument alone carries limited force. Effective correction engages the underlying fears that shape alignment—fear of exclusion, fear of domination, fear of moral displacement.

Tracing this pipeline does not settle political disagreement. It clarifies why many disputes feel irresolvable: they have shifted from deliberation to boundary maintenance, operating on ideas that were never designed to sustain that role.

These cases serve as diagnostics rather than prescriptions. The final part of the book treats the model as an instrument, outlining how to apply it without converting diagnosis into a new form of status signaling.

CHAPTER 18

Organizations & KPI Pipelines

When Intent Becomes a Number

This case examines how drift accelerates when a claim becomes embedded in institutional process, where enforcement and legitimacy pressures reshape function faster than evidence can correct it.

Organizations rarely fail because they lack intent. They fail because intent degrades as it moves.

Leadership goals typically begin as directional claims. They describe what an organization is trying to accomplish and the conditions under which that accomplishment remains legitimate: improve customer trust, reduce friction without sacrificing quality, scale responsibly. These goals are intentionally under-specified. They rely on judgment rather than enumeration. Their accuracy depends on constraints that are understood implicitly rather than written down exhaustively.

At the point of origin, this vagueness is a feature. It allows leaders to adapt intent to local conditions and edge cases. It keeps outcomes, rather than procedures, in view.

The problem emerges as intent begins to travel.

Directional claims do not move cleanly through large organizations. They cannot be easily aggregated, compared, or audited across teams, regions, and time horizons. To coordinate action and evaluate performance, organizations translate intent into measurable proxies. This translation is introduced not as a replacement for judgment, but as a practical necessity.

Over time, however, the proxy begins to stand in for the goal itself.

This chapter traces how organizational intent drifts into KPI regimes—and how those regimes come to govern behavior even when they undermine the outcomes they were meant to support. The focus is not on cynicism or bad actors. It is on how measurement adapts under pressure, and how organizations slowly come to optimize for what can be counted rather than for what was meant.

WHY ORGANIZATIONAL CLAIMS DRIFT SO RELIABLY

Several structural features make organizations unusually fertile environments for drift.

First, organizations operate under **legibility pressure**. Leadership decisions depend on summaries that survive aggregation across layers. What cannot be expressed cleanly in a dashboard or report struggles to influence action, regardless of its importance.

Second, organizations operate under **cadence pressure**. Performance is reviewed weekly, monthly, or quarterly. This rhythm favors metrics that show frequent, incremental movement. Outcomes that materialize slowly, diffusely, or outside the reporting window struggle to compete for attention.

Third, organizations operate under **incentive coupling**. Metrics become tied to compensation, promotion, headcount, and survival. Once a number is linked to reward or punishment, it acquires gravity. People adapt to it.

Fourth, organizations experience **cross-layer context collapse**. Metrics designed at one level are interpreted and acted upon at another—often by people with different constraints, risks, and time horizons. Intent thins as it crosses these layers.

Finally, organizations face **auditability pressure**. What can be defended in review—what can be pointed to, graphed, and explained—outcompetes what is merely true. Measurement becomes a form of protection.

None of these pressures distort intent immediately. They reshape, gradually, which parts of intent remain actionable.

THE ORIGINAL INTENT

In customer service organizations, the originating claim is widely shared and rarely controversial:

Customer support exists to resolve customer problems in a way that restores trust and reduces the likelihood of future contact.

This claim is not vague. It carries clear constraints.

Resolution implies understanding the customer's issue, not merely processing an interaction. Success includes prevention— fixing underlying causes where possible, or at least routing information upstream so problems do not recur. Speed matters, but not at the expense of accuracy, clarity, or durability. Repeat contact is treated as a signal of incomplete resolution rather than as demand to be processed.

Within leadership narratives, service charters, and onboarding materials, these constraints remain visible. The goal is framed as helping customers, not merely handling volume. Judgment remains central. Action is evaluated against outcomes.

This is the claim before it is optimized for travel.

TRANSLATION INTO METRICS

As support operations scale, the origin claim is translated into measurable artifacts.

- Average handle time.
- First-contact resolution.
- Tickets closed per agent.
- Queue time.
- SLA compliance.

These metrics are attractive because they are legible. They allow leaders to compare teams, forecast staffing needs, and demonstrate operational control. They appear as indicators—ways of observing performance rather than defining it.

But the act of measurement introduces compression.

What survives the translation is procedural closure. A ticket can be marked resolved. A call can be ended. A queue can be cleared.

What begins to fall away are the constraints that made the original claim accurate: whether the customer understood the solution, whether the issue was correctly diagnosed, whether the fix prevented recurrence, whether the interaction restored trust.

Resolution becomes a state change in a system rather than an outcome in a customer's experience.

No one needs to abandon the original goal for this to happen. It is enough that reporting systems privilege what they can reliably capture. Over time, what is captured becomes what is discussed. What is discussed becomes what is managed.

WHEN METRICS BECOME EXPLANATIONS

As extracted metrics circulate through regular reporting cycles, they consolidate into a shared internal understanding of performance.

A folk explanation emerges: *if handle time is low and resolution rates are high, customer support is functioning well.*

This explanation is not adopted because it is philosophically compelling. It is adopted because it simplifies coordination. It produces a clear answer to the question, *"How are we doing?"*

As this frame stabilizes, information that does not fit it becomes harder to integrate. Repeat contacts are reinterpreted as customer behavior rather than system failure. Complex issues are reframed as outliers. Time spent investigating root causes appears inefficient because it delays closure.

The dashboard replaces the customer journey as the primary

object of attention.

At this point, the metric no longer functions merely as an indicator. It functions as an explanation. The organization has not decided to value speed over help. It has adapted to a system in which speed is visible and help, in its fuller sense, is not.

WHEN FLUENCY BECOMES STATUS

Once a metric functions as an explanation, it begins to organize rank.

Agents are compared by handle time. Teams by closure rates. Managers by throughput and SLA compliance. What began as observation becomes evaluation.

Competence is inferred not from judgment or durable outcomes, but from metric fluency—the ability to move numbers in the right direction and narrate that movement convincingly.

This produces a predictable behavioral gradient.

Time spent diagnosing systemic issues carries a visible cost. Escalating upstream defects produces little immediate credit. Procedural closure produces immediate, legible gains.

Adaptive behaviors follow. Tickets are phrased to qualify as resolved. Customers are steered toward outcomes that satisfy reporting criteria. Ambiguous issues are routed toward self-service regardless of fit.

These behaviors are rarely experienced as gaming. They are rational responses to an environment that rewards certain outputs reliably and penalizes others quietly.

Resistance begins to carry social cost. Agents who slow down to ensure understanding appear inefficient. Their work is harder to defend in review. Status sorts accordingly.

THE BOUNDARY HARDENS

As the system stabilizes, the metric regime acquires normative force.

Fast agents are praised as strong performers. High-throughput teams are described as disciplined. Low handle times are celebrated as customer-centric, even as repeat contact rises.

Questioning the metrics begins to register as misalignment rather than analysis. Advocating for prevention is reframed as scope creep. Raising concerns about customer frustration sounds like excuse-making when dashboards remain green.

A boundary forms between those who "understand how the system works" and those who do not.

The system does not require explicit enforcement. Career incentives, peer comparison, and performance rituals do the work. Certain concerns stop traveling safely.

At this point, the organization no longer optimizes for helping customers in a durable way. It optimizes for appearing efficient at helping customers.

The system locks.

WHY KPI PIPELINES LOCK IN

Several reinforcing mechanisms raise exit costs.

Prevention is costly upfront and rewarding later, often outside the reporting line that paid for it. Metrics attach directly to careers. Tooling reinforces procedural closure. Leadership narratives commit publicly to improvement stories that become expensive to revise.

The metrics are no longer measurements. They are infrastructure.

Where Drift Could Have Been Slowed

This degradation is not inevitable.

Speed metrics could have traveled alongside repeat-contact indicators. Root-cause work could have counted as performance rather than delay. Managers could have been rewarded for reducing total customer effort over time.

Most importantly, metrics could have been treated as provisional—audited not only for movement, but for whether they still tracked the original intent.

These interventions do not require better people. They require lowering the cost of carrying the original constraints and raising the cost of ignoring them.

Once a proxy becomes identity, correction is difficult.

Before that point, it is an engineering problem.

What the Cases Demonstrate

Part IV applies the model to make the underlying mechanism visible.

Across four domains—health, psychology, politics, and organizations—the surface material varies, while the structural transformations recur. A bounded claim begins inside a context capable of carrying its constraints. It is compressed into an extract that can travel. Extracts consolidate into a story that provides explanatory closure. That story takes on a social function, sorting participants and coordinating behavior. Over time, revision grows expensive as exit acquires social, reputational, or institutional cost.

Taken together, the cases reveal four recurring patterns.

First, drift follows a direction.

Under stable pressures, claims shed constraints in a consistent sequence. Qualifiers and boundary conditions tend to fall away early as transmission costs rise. Substrate gives way to symbolic stand-ins. Falsifiers become harder to articulate and increasingly risky to invoke. By the time a claim stabilizes in public circulation, its factual accuracy may still be debated, but its structural form has already shifted in predictable ways.

This pattern appears regardless of whether the claim concerns hormones, diagnoses, political principles, or organizational goals.

Second, the most consequential changes occur at transitions.

What matters is less the content of belief than the function a claim comes to serve.

- As a claim becomes an extract, portability begins to outweigh fidelity.
- As extracts assemble into a folk theory, coherence begins to outweigh uncertainty.

- As a folk theory becomes a status engine, fluency begins to outweigh understanding.

- As a status engine stabilizes as identity or infrastructure, loyalty begins to outweigh revision.

Each transition marks a durable shift in what the system rewards. Once a claim crosses one of these thresholds, the likelihood of the next failure mode increases—not because anyone decides to abandon accuracy, but because different traits are now being selected for.

Third, resistance to correction emerges from cost rather than weakness.

Early in the pipeline, revision primarily requires effort and attention. Later, it requires social or institutional risk.

Once a claim organizes rank, updating it threatens status. When it organizes belonging, updating it threatens membership. When it organizes incentives, evaluation, or resource access, updating it threatens livelihood.

New information is no longer evaluated solely for truth value, but for consequence: What would changing my position cost me here? Across domains, persistence tracks the relative price of staying versus leaving. When exit costs exceed revision costs, accuracy loses its coordinating role.

This dynamic expresses itself differently in each case:

- In **health pipelines,** beliefs become embodied as routines, purchases, and long-term self-investments.

- In **psychology pipelines**, frameworks provide moral shelter through shared language and group identity.

- In **political pipelines**, positions function as boundary markers under visibility and threat.

- In **organizational pipelines**, proxies harden into infrastructure, shaping incentives and evaluation even when they misalign with original intent.

Across contexts, the mechanism is the same: once a claim becomes load-bearing, correction must contend not with belief alone, but with what the claim now supports.

Fourth, the model's descriptive posture expands its usefulness.

None of the audits rely on diagnosing motive. Drift emerges from ordinary, often reasonable adaptations to incentive structures and environmental pressures. Well-intentioned participants, acting competently within their local contexts, can produce the same outcomes as bad actors.

This is not a moral absolution; it is an analytical advantage. By focusing on mechanics rather than blame, the model generalizes across domains and remains usable in institutional settings, where explanation benefits from clarity without personalization.

Taken together, the cases clarify the purpose of the model. It is not primarily a tool for judging beliefs, but for identifying the point at which a claim shifts from a bounded proposition into social or institutional infrastructure. The practical question becomes not only, *"Is this claim accurate?"*, but, *"What are the cognitive, social, and organizational costs of making it updateable again?"*

That question sets the stage for the final part of the book.

The Toolkit

Part V presents the Drift Model as an instrument. Its purpose is auditability: the ability to locate the stage a claim is operating in, identify the pressures shaping it, and select interventions that preserve constraint fidelity without converting diagnosis into a status display.

This section adopts a procedural stance. It offers methods for identifying claim bundles, locating stages by function rather than by intent, and writing or deciding under uncertainty when time is limited. It also specifies the operating conditions under which the model remains effective, clarifying how its use shapes outcomes in practice.

The guiding discipline is straightforward. Use the model to restore correction capacity by lowering the cost of accuracy and reopening update pathways. Apply it in ways that support revision, proportionality, and continued learning across stages.

CHAPTER 19

How to Use This Model Well

The Drift Model functions as an audit instrument. Its value lies in describing how claims behave under pressure and in helping users orient themselves to the forces shaping transmission, stabilization, and revision.

This chapter establishes the operating posture for everything that follows. It sets the conditions under which the model remains useful and clarifies the discipline required to apply it constructively.

At its core, the practice is straightforward: treat claims as objects, treat environments as pressures, and treat outputs as provisional. When analysis remains revisable without social cost, the instrument is working as intended.

AUDITABILITY AS THE OPERATING POSTURE

The Drift Model is designed to make claims auditable under constraint.

Many public disagreements persist because participants are responding to different versions of the same idea. One person engages with a bounded claim as it exists within a serious tradition. Another responds to a compressed extract, a loyalty signal, or an identity marker derived from it. Interaction escalates because the underlying objects differ.

The model intervenes by shifting attention to structure. Instead of evaluating conclusions directly, it asks how the claim changed as it moved through the environment. Where did qualifiers fall away? At what point did probability harden into certainty? What function does the claim now serve?

This posture changes the interaction. Analysis becomes a tracing exercise rather than a contest. The task is to locate transitions where constraints weakened and to understand the pressures that produced those changes.

Applied this way, the model supports repair by clarifying where fidelity was lost and where correction might still be possible.

COMMON FAILURE PATTERNS

Because the model is compact and portable, it benefits from clear handling discipline.

One common pattern treats stages as indicators of personal sophistication. Used this way, the model becomes a ranking device rather than a diagnostic tool. The stages describe environmental pressure and social cost, not intelligence or character.

Another pattern uses diagnostic language as a rhetorical shortcut. Terms such as "folk theory" or "competence theater" acquire signaling value when deployed against others. At that point, analysis shifts into performance.

A third pattern centers on public diagnosis. Applying the model to strangers or adversaries in visible settings tends to increase identity entanglement and accelerate lock-in rather than clarify structure.

A fourth pattern substitutes labeling for engagement. When stage language is used to bypass evidence rather than examine constraints, certainty increases without calibration.

Each pattern redirects the model from auditability toward dominance.

STAGE-APPROPRIATE INTERVENTION

Effective use of the model depends on matching intervention to stage.

In early stages, claims still function primarily as information. Context, evidence, and restored qualifiers can shift understanding. Pointing to original sources or reintroducing scope often has effect.

At Stage 3, claims operate as narratives. Correction requires an alternative explanation that addresses the same anxiety or uncertainty while preserving complexity.

At Stages 4 and 5, claims function socially. Status and belonging dominate. Here, factual correction alone carries limited leverage. Intervention focuses on reducing performance pressure, lowering exit costs, and creating settings where revision is socially viable.

Diagnosing stage therefore precedes strategy. The same move produces different outcomes depending on the function the claim currently serves.

CONSENT AND ESCALATION

The model works best under conditions of consent.

Collaborative framing invites shared inquiry. Questions such as *"Can we trace how this claim changed from the original study?"* open space for joint analysis.

Public diagnosis, by contrast, raises stakes. Attributing someone's position to hidden motives or signaling function shifts attention from claims to identity. The result is often defensive consolidation rather than revision.[9]

In adversarial environments, the model serves primarily as an internal compass. It helps users decide where effort is likely to be effective and where conditions favor disengagement. Analysis remains informative even when it stays private.

WHAT EFFECTIVE USE LOOKS LIKE

When applied with discipline, the model recedes into the work.

---

9   Karen Frost-Arnold, *Who Should We Be Online? A Social Epistemology for the Internet* (New York: Oxford University Press, 2022), chapters on epistemic responsibility, online agency, and norms that do not reduce everything to intent.

A researcher encountering a viral claim traces it back to the origin bundle, notices a dropped scope condition, and restores the constraint in their summary.

An editor reviewing a headline recognizes a Stage 2 extract, checks the underlying study type, and adjusts framing to preserve accuracy despite lower engagement.

A manager observing a discussion drifting toward identity lock-in alters the environment—moving the conversation into smaller, lower-pressure settings where revision becomes feasible.

In each case, the model shapes decisions without becoming the focus.

The Prime Constraint

The tools that follow sharpen attention. They clarify confusion and support de-escalation. They also increase the risk of performative use.

The model remains effective when it improves the quality of disagreement and expands room for revision. Its signal of success is cleaner argument, not personal elevation.

Operator's Orientation

Applied with care, the model supports disciplined attention:

- Focus on claims rather than people.
- Trace how an idea changed rather than who holds it.
- Match intervention to stage and pressure.
- Restore constraints where they were lost.
- Prefer private analysis when trust is low.

Used this way, the model remains an instrument for understanding rather than a mechanism for sorting.

The distinction is behavioral rather than technical. The work of using the model well consists largely in maintaining that posture.

CHAPTER 20

What Counts as a Claim (and What Doesn't)

Public arguments often collapse at the object level.

The participants enter the discussion holding different kinds of things. One person is working with a bounded proposition: a policy outcome, a causal claim, a prediction with identifiable failure conditions. The other is working with what the issue symbolizes— loyalty, morality, belonging, personal worth. One brings a spreadsheet. The other brings a flag. They talk past each other because the two objects invite different forms of engagement.

Effective use of the Drift Model begins earlier than rebuttal. It begins with object identification. This chapter defines the unit of currency.

THE OBJECT PROBLEM

In high-drift environments, many utterances take the grammatical shape of claims—X is Y—while functioning as a different kind of object. They carry social meaning more than testable content. They do work through signaling, alignment, or boundary maintenance rather than through revisable description.

Treating these objects as standard claims produces predictable outcomes. Time is spent on fact-checking something that was never offered for evaluation. The exchange shifts from inquiry to defense, because the object under discussion carries identity weight. The interaction escalates while the underlying disagreement stays untouched.

Most interventions therefore begin with classification. The first question is simple: *"Is this an object that supports testing, bounding, and revision?"*

THE CLAIM BUNDLE

A workable claim rarely arrives as a single sentence. It arrives as a bundle: a set of interlocking parts that rise or fall together. When these elements are present, the object supports analysis. When they are absent, the object behaves differently.

At minimum, a claim bundle includes:

- **A proposition**: the headline assertion.
- **A scope**: where and when the proposition applies.
- **Constraints**: the limits and assumptions that prevent overreach.
- **A substrate**: the kind of evidence or reasoning doing the work.
- **Falsifiers**: the conditions that would require revision or abandonment.

Public discourse usually presents the proposition alone. The rest of the bundle falls away as transmission cost is reduced. The practical move is to locate what remains of the bundle. Curiosity in response to those missing parts often indicates a claim-like object. Defensive escalation often indicates a different function.

THREE FAST TESTS

Full reconstruction is not always practical. In live settings, three quick probes usually distinguish a claim from other assertion-shaped objects.

Boundedness. Claims have edges. They apply under conditions. They contain failure zones. When an assertion expands to cover all cases and resists any attempt to name limits, it begins functioning as doctrine rather than description.

Support. The question here concerns substrate: what kind of thing does the work? Empirical data, lived experience, logic, and narrative all count as substrates when they are identifiable. "It's obvious" and "everyone knows" provide social confirmation rather than examinable support.

Revisability. Imagine introducing disconfirming evidence. Would revision feel like information gained, or like standing lost? Claims treat error as informative. Load-bearing objects treat error as threat. When revision carries high social cost, the object functions as infrastructure for identity or rank rather than as a proposition.

COMMON NON-CLAIMS

Drift environments produce assertion-shaped objects at scale. Several recurring forms become easy to recognize.

Vibe-as-fact. Statements such as "This city is toxic" use objective grammar to express subjective experience. Their meaning lives in felt perception. The object offers little in the way of falsifiers, because it functions as a report of experience rather than a testable description.

Identity pledge. Phrases like "I believe in science" or "I stand for freedom" operate as badges. They convey affiliation and values. Their primary function is belonging.

Moralized definition. Definitions can be framed so that disagreement becomes moral failure by construction. "Real patriotism means supporting this bill" uses the definition itself to enforce a conclusion. The argument is embedded in the premise.

Narrative smuggling. Two facts are placed side by side with an implied causal glue. "He's a banker, so of course he opposes regulation." The causal claim stays implicit, which keeps it insulated from direct evaluation.

Each of these objects can be coherent and socially useful. Their function differs from revision-oriented epistemic work.

A WORKED EXAMPLE

A single topic can appear as multiple object types.

A well-formed claim about AI risk specifies an architecture, a limitation, and a failure condition. It invites testing. It supports revision.

A drifted version expands scope and sheds constraints: "AI can't be trusted to do real work." The object now behaves more like a folk theory. It points at something real, while its edges dissolve.

A further transformation—"AI is theft"—functions primarily as a moral verdict presented in definitional form. Its role is alignment rather than description, and it draws its force from boundary maintenance rather than empirical structure.

Each object resembles the others on the surface. Only one behaves like a claim bundle.

THE DISCIPLINE

This produces a central discipline for using the model: treat falsifiers as the signature of epistemic objects.

When disconfirming conditions can be named, the object supports inquiry. When they cannot be named, the object supports alignment and boundary work. Alignment plays a legitimate role in human life—values, bonds, loyalties, and identity formation. Clarity comes from distinguishing that role from revision-oriented reasoning.

In high-stakes conversations, the first task is object verification. Establish that both parties are holding the same kind of thing. Locate scope, constraints, substrate, and conditions of failure. When those elements remain unavailable, the most productive move is often a change of posture: from correction to clarification, from argument to boundary recognition, or from engagement to exit.

A claim bundle can be repaired. An assertion-shaped signal calls for a different response.

CHAPTER 21

Locating the Stage a Claim Is In

With the model established, the next task is orientation.

When a claim appears in circulation—a viral post, a heated Slack exchange, a political slogan—the natural impulse is to evaluate its correctness. That impulse makes sense. Accuracy matters. But in environments shaped by drift, correctness alone rarely determines how a claim functions.

Before engaging, it helps to locate the object. The same sentence can behave very differently depending on context. It may be carrying information forward. It may be signaling competence. Or it may be holding a boundary in place.

This chapter provides a way to make that distinction. It offers an orientation tool for calibrating response to environment rather than to surface content.

FUNCTION RATHER THAN INTENT

A common early mistake is to treat drift as a question of motive.

Distorted claims often invite assumptions about deception or manipulation. Yet in high-pressure environments, intent explains little. A speaker can be entirely sincere while operating a Stage 4 status engine. The belief may be genuine even as the form and timing of its expression serve a social function.

Using the model effectively means shifting attention away from mind-reading and toward mechanics. Instead of asking what the speaker believes internally, ask what repeating the claim accomplishes in this setting.

- Does it advance understanding of a mechanism?
- Does it display fluency, sharpness, or moral seriousness?

- Does it signal safety, loyalty, or alignment?

A claim is defined by its function in the moment. The same words can operate as a tentative hypothesis in one environment and as a loyalty marker in another. Analysis begins with the job the claim is performing.

THE CORE INSTRUMENT

Locating a claim's stage rarely requires elaborate tools. In most situations, three questions provide sufficient clarity.

The first concerns **function**. What does the claim do here? Does it transmit information? Offer a unifying explanation? Sort participants into insiders and outsiders? Or reinforce a boundary under perceived threat?

The second concerns **reward**. What does repeating the claim provide to the speaker? In early stages, the reward is often understanding or correction. In extraction phases, it may be attention. In status dynamics, it is recognition—appearing sharp, aligned, or serious. In identity systems, the reward is security: remaining inside the boundary.

The third concerns **revision cost**. Consider what would follow if the speaker publicly revised the claim. In some environments, revision earns respect or invites discussion. In others, it carries embarrassment, loss of standing, or social risk. When revision entails meaningful loss, the claim has moved beyond information.

Together, these questions—function, reward, and revision cost— usually locate the stage with surprising reliability.

STAGE SIGNATURES

Once oriented, each environment tends to reveal a recognizable signature.

In **serious traditions**, claims move slowly and carry their constraints. Qualifiers are explicit. Scope is narrow. The primary concern centers on calibration and error.

Meme extracts travel lightly. They emphasize speed and recognizability. Nuance gives way to portability, and edge cases recede from view.

Folk theories provide closure. Fragments assemble into a story that explains events and experience. The emotional reward lies in coherence and relief.

Status engines introduce competition. Language sharpens. Insider terms proliferate. Fluency and certainty signal rank within the group.

Identity systems organize belonging. Moral language dominates. Boundaries become salient. The central concern shifts toward safety within the group.

These stages describe functional patterns rather than moral categories.

COMMON MISREADINGS

Certain confusions recur when emotions run high.

High visibility is often mistaken for deep commitment. A claim can circulate widely while remaining loosely held by many participants. Treating casual engagement as identity investment raises stakes unnecessarily.

Status performances are also frequently read as conviction. Stage 4 dynamics can appear intense while remaining oriented toward recognition rather than belief. Responses aimed at persuasion often miss the audience the performance addresses.

Coherence is sometimes treated as evidence. Folk theories feel compelling because they hang together. That internal consistency produces confidence, even when the explanation has drifted from underlying reality.

DIAGNOSTIC DISCIPLINE

Stage assessment always remains provisional.

Observation occurs from the outside. Signals are visible; private doubts and side conversations are not. For that reason, diagnostic language functions best when it describes dynamics rather than assigns conditions.

Framing matters. Saying "this exchange carries high exit costs" identifies a structure. Saying "you are trapped in an identity system" assigns a role. The first improves accuracy. The second narrows it.

This discipline supports the model's purpose. Bounded diagnosis preserves calibration and avoids converting analysis into performance.

CHOOSING WHEN TO APPLY THE TOOL

This framework is designed primarily for orientation—clarifying how an environment works and where leverage exists.

In public or adversarial settings, internal use often proves most effective. Applying diagnostic labels outwardly tends to raise stakes rather than lower them, as such labels are received as judgments about character.

Understanding the stage clarifies where engagement helps, where it distracts, and where restraint preserves optionality. In many cases, insight lies in recognizing where pressure operates and adjusting behavior accordingly.

Knowing the stage reveals both where movement is possible and where patience serves better than force.

CHAPTER 22

Seeing the Environment: Why Pressures Matter More Than Motives

When a claim drifts—when a scientific finding condenses into a slogan, or a political argument settles into a loyalty marker— the most immediate questions tend to focus on people. Who is speaking? What are they trying to do? What do they want others to believe?

These are questions about motive. They offer clarity by supplying a protagonist. They also narrow the frame. In large systems, individual intent is often overshadowed by incentives. Outcomes emerge from selection processes that operate regardless of intention, shaping what persists and what fades.

To understand why a bird has a curved beak, attention shifts away from preference and toward habitat. The relevant questions concern available food, environmental constraints, and the pressures that reward one shape over another. Claims evolve in much the same way.

This chapter develops that shift in perspective: from interpreting speakers to reading the environment that selects among what they say.

WHY ENVIRONMENT COMES FIRST

Drift follows a pattern of adaptation.

Claims change shape as they move through environments that reward certain properties and penalize others. When an environment favors speed over deliberation, certainty over nuance, and clarity over calibration, the variants that thrive will reflect those priorities.

Intended meaning becomes secondary to structural fit. Elements that increase carrying cost—qualifiers, scope conditions, uncertainty—gradually fall away. Elements that improve aerodynamics—slogans, villains, moral clarity—gain lift.

Looking through the lens of motive reveals a world organized around character. Looking through the lens of pressure reveals a world organized around adaptation.

For drift diagnosis, the container shapes outcomes more reliably than the content.

FOUR PRESSURES YOU CAN OBSERVE DIRECTLY

Understanding the pressures acting on a claim does not require access to internal systems or proprietary logic. Most environments express their incentives through a small number of visible forces.

Attention pressure functions as a clock. Time is scarce, and processing speed matters. Claims that deliver a fast payoff—novelty, emotional charge, immediate clarity—move more easily through this environment. Under high attention pressure, compression accelerates. The felt experience is urgency: complexity slows movement.

Distribution pressure functions as a megaphone. Visibility depends on routing systems that amplify engagement. Conflict generates more interaction than agreement. Polarization produces stronger signals than calibration. Under high distribution pressure, claims gravitate toward formats that reliably provoke response. The felt experience is amplification: salience determines reach.

Context collapse functions as a stage. Multiple audiences—friends, colleagues, critics, strangers—occupy the same visibility field. Speech adapts by prioritizing defensibility. Ambiguity narrows. Exploration yields to declaration. The felt experience is exposure: clarity protects against misreading by the most demanding listener.

Enforceability pressure functions as a rulebook. Governance at scale depends on legibility. Systems rely on categories that can be recognized, classified, and acted upon. Moral language travels well here because it maps cleanly onto rules and enforcement. The felt experience is compliance: framing shapes survivability.

These pressures operate as constraints. Their effects are visible in what spreads, what stabilizes, and what disappears.

How Pressures Drive Stage Transitions

Once a dominant pressure becomes legible, the direction of drift often follows.

When attention pressure intensifies, Stage 1 claims tend to move toward Stage 2 extraction. Dense bundles give way to lighter forms that travel more easily.

When distribution pressure dominates, Stage 2 fragments consolidate into Stage 3 folk theories. Coherent narratives sustain engagement more effectively than isolated pieces.

When context collapse intensifies, Stage 3 theories evolve into Stage 4 status engines. Public clarity and visible fluency become efficient signals in mixed-audience settings.

When enforceability pressure rises, Stage 4 contests settle into Stage 5 identity systems. Boundaries sharpen, rules formalize, and revision costs increase.

This pattern does not determine every outcome, but it appears frequently enough to guide analysis and intervention.

Reading the Environment

Active pressures announce themselves through surface signals.

High attention pressure shortens cycles. Claims rise and fall rapidly. Demand centers on immediacy and simplification.

High distribution pressure compresses language. Qualifiers

shrink. Headlines drift away from underlying evidence as consolidation becomes advantageous.

High enforceability pressure increases moral framing. Technical disagreements translate into categorical terms such as harm, safety, or violation. Speech aligns with what systems can process.

High context collapse makes exit costs visible. People adjust visibility, hedge language, compartmentalize audiences, or shift accounts. Speech adapts to adversarial conditions.

These signals reveal what an environment rewards and what it discourages.

FROM ATTRIBUTION TO ARCHITECTURE

This shift in perspective opens a different set of possibilities.

When drift is understood as a product of individual character, responses focus on exposure, condemnation, or reform. Those approaches scale poorly. Large systems rarely stabilize through changes in motive alone.

When drift is understood as a product of mechanics—claims adapting to selection pressures—interventions target structure. Formats can change. Routing can shift. Friction can be added where distortion is cheap and reduced where accuracy is heavy. Exit costs can be lowered. Correction pathways can widen.

Drift emerges wherever incentives align. Reduction follows when environments are redesigned to support calibration.

Architecture, not attribution, determines what persists.

CHAPTER 23

Reducing Drift Without Persuasion

The book has focused on diagnosis. This chapter turns to repair.

Repair begins with a shift in stance. Instead of approaching drift as a problem of belief, it treats drift as a property of systems. Rather than centering argument, it centers design. Rather than changing minds directly, it changes the conditions under which claims move.

When people encounter a drifted claim—a slogan standing in for a study, a folk theory standing in for explanation, a belief functioning as identity—the instinct is engagement. Data is presented. Fallacies are named. Positions harden. Under pressure, this pattern raises defenses and increases the social cost of revision.

A different approach proves more reliable. Claims are treated as objects moving through channels. Attention shifts from persuasion to transmission.

TRANSMISSION AS THE UNIT OF CHANGE

The Drift Model reframes how information behaves in public systems.

Claims carry complexity, encounter friction, and gain or lose velocity depending on their environment. When constraints fall away in Stage 2, the cause often lies in channel capacity rather than sender intent. When claims stabilize as identity in Stage 5, the cause often lies in revision cost rather than cognitive ability.

This reframing directs attention away from motive and toward infrastructure. The relevant question becomes how to lower the cost of accuracy and how to make revision survivable.

FOUR LEVERS THAT MATTER

A small number of interventions consistently produce outsized effects. Each operates on transmission conditions rather than on belief.

Make constraints easy to carry.

Nuance often drops because it is packaged separately from the claim. Scope conditions and caveats appear deep in supporting material while the headline circulates on its own. Constraint preservation improves when limits travel with the claim itself. Scope boxes on slides, confidence intervals in headlines, and visible applicability notes ensure that movement carries boundaries alongside conclusions.

Make distortion costly.

Drift accelerates when context separates from content at low effort. Introducing friction changes the calculus. Required links to primary sources, prompts that encourage reading before sharing, and organizational norms that anchor decisions to underlying material all raise the energy cost of separation. The effect is structural: claims retain their substrate longer.

Route claims into bounded containers.

Many failures arise from venue mismatch. Context collapse turns fragile claims into performances. Routing addresses this by matching complexity to space. Sensitive or technical issues benefit from environments with defined membership, shared norms, and reduced audience pressure. When the container fits the claim, revision becomes easier.

Make revision survivable.

Identity lock-in forms when updating carries social risk. Incentives shape this outcome. Systems that reward early correction, recognize uncertainty, and treat updates as competence signals lower exit costs. Rituals that celebrate course correction reshape the meaning of being wrong.

MATCHING INTERVENTIONS TO STAGE

Effective repair aligns tools with stage.

Upstream—Stages 1 through 3—claims remain fluid. Here, structural support matters most. Better formats, clearer documentation, visible constraints, and routing decisions shape what circulates and how faithfully it travels.

Downstream—Stages 4 and 5—claims operate primarily as social instruments. Here, de-escalation becomes the dominant move. Changes to venue, reductions in audience size, and lowered stakes reopen space for revision. In these environments, evidence functions best when paired with social safety.

THE SCOPE OF DRIFT REDUCTION

Drift reduction focuses on fidelity and correction capacity.

When claims carry their limits, evidence remains visible, and revision preserves standing, the system supports accurate disagreement. Differences of view can persist without escalating into identity conflict. The objective is durability rather than consensus.

WHAT THIS LOOKS LIKE IN PRACTICE

The most effective interventions are ordinary.

- A team adds a "Where this applies" and "Where this breaks" section to every proposal, and strategies gain precision.

- A moderator routes a volatile discussion into a smaller, slower forum with sourcing norms, and problem-solving replaces performance.

- An organization recognizes leaders who revise direction early, and updating acquires positive social meaning.

Each change alters what is cheap, what is costly, and what feels safe.

CUMULATIVE EFFECTS

Systems respond to small adjustments.

Constraint preserved early prevents hardening later. A clarification added in Stage 2 reduces the likelihood of identity entanglement in Stage 5. Each design choice compounds across the pipeline.

This is the logic of engineering: modest interventions, placed at the right point, reshape outcomes over time.

CHAPTER 24

Writing and Deciding Under Uncertainty

The previous chapter examined infrastructure. This one turns to craft.

Institutional writing—memos, decks, briefs, roadmaps—plays a central role in how organizations think and act. These documents translate uncertainty into shared understanding and coordinated action. They also shape how beliefs travel inside institutions and beyond them.

Many professional norms emphasize confidence, alignment, and narrative clarity. Writers are trained to present a decisive arc toward action, to smooth disagreement, and to compress uncertainty into footnotes or appendices. These habits produce documents that feel strong and read smoothly. They also produce claims that travel easily once they leave their original context.

To manage drift, organizations benefit from a different writing discipline—one that supports action under uncertainty while preserving the ability to revise. This chapter outlines practical techniques for doing that work.

SEPARATE THE CLAIM, THE CONFIDENCE, AND THE DECISION

Clear writing under uncertainty begins with disentangling belief from action.

In professional documents, claims and decisions often appear in the same sentence:

> *"Because AI will revolutionize our industry, we are investing $10 million."*

This structure feels efficient because it compresses reasoning and response. It also binds the action to the belief in a way that raises the cost of revision. When belief and decision move together, later updates to understanding place pressure on the original judgment rather than on the evolving evidence.

A more resilient structure separates the bundle.

Every serious document can distinguish three elements:

- **The claim**: the proposition about the world.
- **The confidence**: the current level of certainty and its basis.
- **The decision**: the action taken in response.

For example:

"Our working hypothesis is that AI will materially reshape this industry. Our confidence is medium, given unresolved regulatory risk and uncertain customer adoption. Given the potential downside of inaction, we are authorizing a $10 million exploratory investment."

This structure creates room for learning. Confidence can change without retroactively recasting the decision as error. The organization acted based on risk management, not certainty. Updating becomes a routine operation rather than a reputational event.

This separation forms the foundation of drift-resistant writing.

TREAT UNCERTAINTY AS AN ASSET

Uncertainty carries operational value when it is visible at the point of decision.

Many documents sequester uncertainty in footnotes or disclaimers. A more effective approach places it near the top of the document, where it can inform judgment directly. One useful tool is an **Uncertainty Register**: a brief section that maps the current state of knowledge.

A functional register distinguishes among four categories:

- **Known**: claims supported by verified substrate such as data, tests, or direct observation.

- **Unknown**: gaps that remain unresolved.

- **Assumed**: propositions treated as true for speed or coordination.

- **Contested**: points of informed disagreement within the team.

This practice accomplishes two things. It makes reasoning legible, and it lowers the cost of correction. When an assumption changes or a gap closes, the document evolves as designed. Learning becomes visible, and foresight is rewarded.

Over time, organizations that adopt this discipline build tolerance for honesty and flexibility.

CITE SUBSTRATE, NOT PRESTIGE

Claims travel more reliably when they remain anchored to their evidentiary base.

Professional writing often relies on authority cues—institutions, titles, or credentials—to convey rigor. A more durable approach describes the work itself rather than the reputation attached to it.

Instead of naming who produced the knowledge, specify what was done:

- a survey of ten thousand nurses,

- a randomized controlled trial in mice,

- a longitudinal analysis over five years,

- a series of interviews with twenty enterprise customers.

This level of detail restores proportionality. It allows readers to assess relevance, scope, and strength without deferring to prestige.

The claim remains connected to its substrate rather than floating as an abstract conclusion.

When evidence can be described concretely, confidence becomes easier to calibrate.

VERSION BELIEFS, NOT JUST DOCUMENTS

Learning becomes visible when organizations track how understanding evolves.

Many teams maintain file versioning while leaving belief changes implicit. A complementary practice records shifts in reasoning directly within the document. A simple belief log can note:

- when the initial hypothesis was formed,
- what evidence adjusted confidence,
- why a pivot occurred,
- what new uncertainty emerged.

This record preserves institutional memory. It distinguishes being updated from being mistaken and allows adaptation to register as competence rather than reversal.

Organizations that remember how they learned are better equipped to respond to change.

NAME THE FALSIFIER

Every operational claim benefits from an explicit test.

A clear sentence completes the structure:

"We will revise this claim if..."

The falsifier can take many forms: a metric threshold, a missing user behavior, a competitor move, or a regulatory change. The requirement is concreteness rather than perfection.

Writing the falsifier in advance creates shared expectations. It signals that revision is part of the plan. When the condition appears, the response is procedural rather than personal.

Documents that include falsifiers invite learning and adjustment as a matter of course.

THE ANTI-DRIFT WRITING RULE

A single principle ties these practices together:

Documents that support revision remain useful over time.

The purpose of writing under uncertainty is to enable action while preserving flexibility. Effective documents provide enough structure to act and enough openness to move as conditions change.

This approach allows organizations to decide without overstating certainty, to act without hardening belief, and to update without loss of standing.

That is how writing supports judgment under pressure—and how drift is kept in check as ideas move through the system.

CHAPTER 25
How This Model Gets Misused

This is the point at which drift analysis turns back on itself.

The tools in this book—the stages, the pressures, the audit protocols—are designed to describe how claims change under pressure. Like any conceptual system, they also travel through social environments. As they circulate, they encounter the same forces they were built to analyze. When constraints fall away, the model can shift function: from diagnostic instrument to identity signal, from analytic aid to social weapon.

This chapter describes how that shift occurs, how misuse appears in practice, and how to recognize the moment when analysis begins to produce the very dynamics it was meant to clarify.

WHEN DIAGNOSTICS BECOME IDENTITY

Analytical frameworks become most fragile when they start signaling belonging.

The shift is audible in everyday language. Stage labels move from describing claim behavior to characterizing people. Terminology becomes shorthand for competence rather than a tool for inquiry. Fluency begins to signal rank.

At that point, the model's function has changed. It no longer examines claims in motion. It sorts participants. What initially felt like insight now performs social work: establishing distance, reinforcing hierarchy, and rewarding certainty.

This transformation follows the same dynamics traced throughout the book. Fluency becomes a signal. Diagnosis becomes performance. The framework stabilizes as a marker of who "gets it," rather than as a means of understanding how drift unfolds.

The Path of Weaponization

Misuse follows a recognizable sequence.

It often begins with vocabulary acquisition. Learning the language of substrate, falsifiers, and exit cost brings precision and clarity. Using the terms correctly feels like progress.

Next comes labeling. Applying a stage classification to a person or group resolves tension efficiently. The label ends discussion faster than engagement with evidence. The terms start functioning as shortcuts.

Over time, evaluation replaces description. Stages become rankings. Early stages acquire positive connotations; later stages take on moral weight. The model shifts from mapping pressure to judging character.

As reputation becomes tied to diagnostic sharpness, revision grows costly. Updating an analysis threatens standing. At this point, criticism is processed as confirmation that the diagnosis was correct. The framework stabilizes as an identity system.

The loop has closed. A diagnostic meant to expose identity formation now sustains one.

Contexts That Amplify Risk

The model interacts differently with different environments.

In adversarial public settings—comment threads, call-out posts, broadcast debates—diagnosis functions as provocation. Analytical language reads as insult, and response patterns tighten accordingly.

In competitive settings, where winning or demonstrating acuity is the primary reward, diagnostic tools accelerate escalation. Raising exit costs hardens positions.

In communities organized around strong boundary enforcement, analytical naming increases visibility and risk. In such contexts, reflection operates more effectively as private orientation than public intervention.

Diagnosis also depends on reconstruction. Tracing a claim back to its origin bundle grounds analysis in structure rather than impression. Without that anchor, classification reflects projection more than audit.

Across all contexts, claims remain the unit of analysis. People hold different claims at different stages simultaneously. Treating individuals as stage-bound entities collapses complexity and accelerates lock-in.

MOVES THAT LOWER PRESSURE

When drift is present, small shifts in interaction can reduce pressure without triggering defense.

Lowering exit cost matters. Acknowledging what resonates before narrowing scope allows revision to feel like refinement rather than surrender.

Containers shape behavior. Moving a discussion from a public arena into a bounded or private setting often dissolves the performance incentives that drive escalation.

Constraints open space. Questions about scope, conditions, or applicability invite calibration without demanding reversal.

Tempo matters. Provisional decisions, small tests, and time-limited commitments prevent beliefs from congealing into identity markers.

These moves operate quietly. Their effectiveness comes from changing conditions rather than naming dynamics.

ORGANIZATIONAL HYGIENE

Groups that use this model benefit from shared discipline.

Diagnostic work fits naturally into debriefs and retrospectives, where reflection is expected and status stakes are lower. Documents provide safer objects of analysis than individuals. Language that tracks scope loss or constraint drift keeps attention on structure.

Norms that surface uncertainty make revision routine. Explicitly valuing updates as competence aligns incentives with learning. Over time, these practices keep analysis directed outward, toward systems and pressures, rather than inward, toward people.

The Test That Matters

The measure of correct use is practical rather than rhetorical.

A well-used model expands room for thought. It makes disagreement cleaner, revision cheaper, and uncertainty speakable. It increases the number of viable next moves.

A misused model narrows that space. It quiets exploration, hardens positions, and rewards display.

The Drift Model does its work when it lowers heat and restores flexibility. When it raises status or sharpens boundaries, it has begun to drift.

Responsibility When Drift Is Predictable

This book has treated drift as a structural phenomenon. Claims change function as they move through environments shaped by attention, incentives, and reuse. Those changes follow regular patterns. They do not require bad intent, persuasion, or error to take hold. They arise from transmission itself.

Once drift is understood this way, responsibility takes on a different shape. It no longer consists in defending claims from change or insisting on perfect transmission. It consists in anticipating how claims will be altered by circulation and deciding, in advance, how they should be carried.

Some claims remain intelligible under reuse. Others do not. Some tolerate compression with little loss. Others change meaning quickly once conditions are stripped away. The difference is not moral. It is functional. Responsibility begins with recognizing which claims belong to which category and designing their movement accordingly.

Across the book, a single distinction has recurred: the difference between a claim that explains and a claim that coordinates. Explanatory claims aim to reduce uncertainty about the world. Coordinating claims aim to align action, identity, or belief. Both are necessary. Confusion arises when one is mistaken for the other, or when a claim shifts function without being recognized as having done so.

Responsibility, in this sense, is a matter of stewardship. It involves preserving the conditions under which explanation remains possible, even as coordination pressures increase. It involves maintaining paths back to bounded versions of claims as derivatives proliferate. It involves keeping revision socially affordable as circulation continues.

Design choices shape these outcomes. Where claims are stabilized, how they are summarized, when they are broadcast, and what constraints are allowed to travel with them all matter. These choices determine whether drift remains legible or becomes invisible, whether correction remains procedural or becomes reputational, and whether learning accumulates or stalls.

The Drift Model does not promise control. It offers orientation. It makes visible the pressures that act on claims once they leave protected contexts and enter shared space. Used well, it expands the room for judgment by clarifying what kind of object a claim has become and what kinds of responses remain available.

That is the responsibility this book points toward: not mastery over discourse, but care in design; not certainty about outcomes, but foresight about pressures; not immunity to drift, but competence in living with it.

This is the work of stewardship in environments where transmission is constant and meaning is shaped by movement.

Bibliography

Benkler, Yochai, Robert Faris, and Hal Roberts. *Network Propaganda: Manipulation, Disinformation, and Radicalization in American Politics*. New York: Oxford University Press, 2018.

Boyd, Danah. *It's Complicated: The Social Lives of Networked Teens*. New Haven: Yale University Press, 2014.

Frost-Arnold, Karen. *Who Should We Be Online? A Social Epistemology for the Internet*. New York: Oxford University Press, 2022.

Gillespie, Tarleton. *Custodians of the Internet: Platforms, Content Moderation, and the Hidden Decisions That Shape Social Media*. New Haven: Yale University Press, 2018.

Noble, Safiya Umoja. *Algorithms of Oppression: How Search Engines Reinforce Racism*. New York: New York University Press, 2018.

Phillips, Whitney, and Ryan M. Milner. *The Ambivalent Internet: Mischief, Oddity, and Antagonism Online*. Cambridge: Polity, 2017.

Shifman, Limor. *Memes in Digital Culture*. Cambridge, MA: MIT Press, 2014.

Wu, Tim. *The Attention Merchants: The Epic Scramble to Get Inside Our Heads*. New York: Knopf, 2016.

Zuboff, Shoshana. *The Age of Surveillance Capitalism: The Fight for a Human Future at the New Frontier of Power*. New York: PublicAffairs, 201

ABOUT THE AUTHORS

Zachary Handa is a search strategist and systems designer specializing in how information becomes visible, trusted, and distorted at scale. His background spans over a decade in digital marketing, including agency work, affiliate program management, and enterprise SEO product leadership at AT&T.

His work focuses on the structural conditions that govern claim transmission across platforms, organizations, and AI systems. He specializes in designing visibility and correction architectures that unify human expertise with machine-readable structure, enabling durable knowledge to remain retrievable and revisable under conditions of scale.

Georg Sinn is the Founder of AllYouCanGET and a Senior Data Solution Architect whose work explores the relationship between digital systems, knowledge formation, and ethical responsibility.

With over two decades of experience in Business Intelligence and Data Governance at organizations such as IBM and Kyndryl, Georg brings deep expertise in software development, data platforms, and information architecture. Beyond technical implementation, he focuses on how data infrastructures shape perception, influence collective understanding, and mediate truth in networked societies.

His work integrates philosophical inquiry with practical consulting, emphasizing transparency, accountability, and human-centered data practices. Through digital strategy, custom communication systems, and governance frameworks, he helps organizations navigate the ethical challenges of information ecosystems. His perspective situates data not merely as a resource to be optimized, but as a cultural and epistemic force, central to understanding how ideas, narratives, and "memes" circulate, evolve, and gain authority in the digital age.

www.ingramcontent.com/pod-product-compliance
Lightning Source LLC
Chambersburg PA
CBHW052136270326
41930CB00012B/2915